A *Matter* FOR TIME

GEORGE ACKER

TABLE OF CONTENTS

IBC

3rd December 1999

Ref:INT/JG

Dear Mr Acker

2000 OUTSTANDING INTELLECTUALS OF THE 20TH CENTURY

The Oxford English Dictionary defines intellectualism as the "doctrine that knowledge is wholly or mainly derived from pure reason" and it follows by saying that an intellectual is a "person possessing a good understanding, enlightened person".

Surely, therefore, this definition is the reason for your selection to be included in this prestigious publication which is due for release in late 2000. I invite you to take your place within its pages. Only two thousand intellectuals can be featured from across the world and I therefore urge you to complete the enclosed questionnaire as soon as possible.

Inclusion is based on merit alone and there is no obligation to purchase a copy of **2000 Outstanding Intellectuals of the 20th Century**. However, I recommend you to study the Reservation Form on the reverse of the enclosed questionnaire and return it to me by the date shown or as soon as possible.

I look forward to receiving your completed questionnaire.

Sincerely

JON GIFFORD
Editor in Chief

International Biographical Centre is an imprint of Melrose Press Ltd. whose offices are at
St Thomas Place, Ely, Cambridgeshire CB7 4GG, England. Registered in England number 966974

INTRODUCTION

"When the people realized it wasn't broken,
they realized it could not be fixed.
It simply did not work."

A Matter for Time

IT IS HIGHLY SUGGESTED that anyone reading this book acquaint themselves with the Glossary first. Many of the words in this book are redefined especially for the reader of this book. It is probable reading this book without understanding the words defined to fit the tone and rhythm of the book will result in either no gain or confusion in the readers understanding of its purpose.

The purpose is to guide believers to Liberation. Attaining Liberation separates a believer from fear of death. When one finds Liberation death is nothing other than another beginning. A liberated person is a Master of Self and no problem to the world, nor is the liberated one troubled by the world.

His or Her belief in the Creator sets a seal on their hearts that renders them incapable of submitting to the wills of any other than the all Mighty, who they serve.

The unprincipled amongst us shall have an empty victory when all believers refuse to give them power by doing as they demand. What profit a group to conquer the land of a people who'd prefer death to cooperating with them.

From the moment a person enters life they begin their exit from life. To allow anyone to teach or instruct, efficiently, fear of an absolute is insane. Departing life is an absolute. Fearing death gives too much power to unprincipled entities. Worst than succumbing to such teachings is dignifying them by revering false and ruthless gangs Kings and Queens, Colonizers, Imperialists, and other Takers. At best they function to obscure the Real Purpose of Human Life.

An age old question that few have found the answer to is what is the meaning of life. Many a Scholar and Erudite have pondered the purpose of it all. To fully understand the answer to the question it is necessary to start at the beginning. By understanding there are no endings just beginnings the answer may be grasped. Each beginning leads to another beginning.

A person's entering life starts the beginning of their exit from life, which is not an ending but another beginning. Simple fact is the better one lives this life, the better they are prepared for the next beginning. It is not complicated, as most have been misled to believe.

The confusion has its origin in insane actions and choices. Insanity may be simply defined as, "None belief in a Creator of this Experience." Sanity may be simply defined as "A belief in a Creator of this Experience. The insane are a kind of the species Man.

In looking at the make up of a kind of Man it becomes apparent his nature is discordant with what exists. He is forever attempting to make this experience what he imagined it would be or should be. He wanted to make it what he wanted. To do this he had to enlist the help of Man. What better device to employ in accomplishing this than to trick Man.

Deliberately this kind of Man began to manipulate the physical world and snare Man. He convinced man that life was about self-indulgence. That seemed to work out just fine. Practice makes perfect and it was no different with the insane man. He sold Man on the idea that it was a good thing to be greedy, deceptive, and irresponsible. Do whatever you want to do is not a hard pill to swallow. That went over well. It was working better than expected. It was then that this kind of man introduced the ruse of 'progress'. Man jumped at it. The insane Man had appealed to the sane Man's lower nature. Man being ignorant of himself thought he was living well and life had no more to offer. What upset the apple cart was the precious few that looked further into life and saw the Truth.

The precious few were the people who did not bend to the insanity of the insane.

Instead they developed faith in a Universal Self and their ability to ascend into it. They were the sane. They knew life was temporary and something, of major importance, was connected to life beyond eating, procreating, fighting, and fleeing. These four things were characteristics of Man's lower nature and hosted Man's immaturity. In time they realized Man had capabilities that far exceeded the function of either mechanical devise, or magical tricks. There was something to acquire that can be taken to the next experience. They also, knew Man alone could obtain this most valuable treasure. It was available to Man in his belief in a Creator of it all. Through his belief came his sanity. His sanity made him Man. It was unavailable to the non believers as they were insane and dedicated to proving there was no Creator. They were a kind of man, and an enemy to Man.

This much we know for certain, from the moment we enter this World we begin our exit from it. Also, we know no matter what we achieve in the world of the temporal it matters little upon our exit. Lastly, we know we are searching for something to give the experience meaning. Apparently what we are in search of is beyond fulfillments of the offerings of the temporal world. It may be we are in search of self, at higher and higher levels of Union with our Creator, the infinite self. It sounds too simple to be True.

That which lies outside the world of definition or description is infinite. Things such as kindness, happiness, Joy, spirit, soul, and peace are members of the infinite. Man is also, a member of the infinite. His dilemma is whether to purse the finite or the infinite in finding self. He must make a choice. No man has ever been able to walk in two different directions at the same time. A step to the East and a step to the West results in no movement at all, stagnation. One cannot find self in motionlessness. One must be active in the unseen world and passive in the seen world. The seen world is not who you are. It is only a stage on which spirit must prevail over matter to realize self in becoming Truth.

Oddly enough what we are searching for is Self. By self is meant that which is ever born and knows being, only. It is ageless and ever transitional. It is colorless and odorless. It is neither male, nor female. It knows all that is seen as well as all that is unseen as self. Self neither lives, nor dies. Self is infinite.

Life is best viewed as a Journey into a dream. It is a journey filled with traps, snares, and distractions to dismay the will of self and misguide the unsuspecting traveler. The successful traveler finds his way to proper guidance and faces himself in finding self. Then the traveler becomes master of self.

The degree of self mastery we attain exits this experience with each person. Self Mastery is the one thing that leaves this experience with each one of us. It stands alone as the ultimate offering of this journey. It prepares us for the higher experiences of being. As one ascends into being it is necessary to have control of ones self. There will be no one to watch over us and maintain the Peace among us at the higher levels of being. We will have to be self governing agents to qualify for entrance into the higher realms of being. This experience affords us an arena in which to practice self government preparation for assimilation into highly developed and evolved beings.

Spiritual Alchemy comes in to the experience by turning the negative things that transpire in ones life into Spiritual Gold. The way is hard for one who is Real. In being sane the insane ones are ever attempting to get believers to abandon their faith and join them in insanity. The non believers are ever making things easy for each other and their agents and making things difficult for the believers. A spiritual alchemist understands the antics of the insane and wades through the indignations anticipating a brighter day. The ignorance of the non believer is evident in their lack of faith. The true spiritual alchemist forgives them for they know not what they do.

The Masters of Self are no trouble to the world nor are Masters troubled by the world. They have found the Peace, that is blissful, beyond all understanding and ever after free from the toil and the tumult of involuntary returning to life. Fore they have overcome life and found themselves in infinity. To the Master a lump of clay and a nugget of gold have the same value. Both are but parts of a restless dream that fades at the coming of each awakening. They are as finite and as empty of content as smoke blown into the wind. The Master knows life to be an empty dream and dreams are for those who sleep. The Masters of Self are awake and operating on 92% of their brains. The Master knows the knower of the known to be the friend. The above is an advantage of the sane.

May the words on these pages find their way into your journey and set your feet on the Path to self and liberation from either life or death.

In truth Man is made in God's image. The image of God is infinite. Man is the only thing in creation in that likeness. Man when he is sane devotes himself to self mastery. It is the development of self mastery that affords man the passage to infinity. Innocence is the most important part of self mastery. It alone is the foundation for union with God.

May the words on these pages serve to lift the weights of self reprisal and self judgment from the shoulders of all who seek. They are simply some of the writings on walls of the Path. They are intended as succulent nutriments for the souls of seekers of Truth. For they who know, in their hearts, shall know the Truth in *that* quiet place inside themselves.

Peace

Chapter

1

A NATION GROWS UP

THE AIR SMELLED SO new and the sounds of nature all around Him blotted out thoughts of the content of the Manuel He had been given upon release from prison. He boarded the bus with His valise, the Manuel, and an 9" x 12" manila envelope. The smells were vastly different in the bus. They conflicted with the fresh air outside. Stale cigarette odor hovered in the air, and all around were discordant scents and fragrances, as each person was drenched in their favorite fragrances and scents. His thoughts switched from the smells and fragrances to the life ahead. For some time He'd been a guest of the state. He did not like the climate of Prison. That part of his life was over. However, the lessons learned would forever stay in the upper recesses of his mind. He realized He did not know what the main purpose of life was. That much had become clear to Him in prison. That was the one thing He had to figure out. One group advocated this was the purpose, another group held a different view. In the midst of all that He had to find the solution. He gathered there were many answers to the question, but one Universal Solution.

Closing all Prisons came as a shock to habitual offenders. It deprived them of their comfort zones. Closing the prisons was supported by documentation of their unsuccessfully fulfilling the designed purpose.

The facts revealed it was a gigantic miss-appropriation of public funds. Far too many of the convicts relied on the Prison System as a mercy and a blessing. Fact was, they looked forward to returning. A quirk of human nature is, 'people like people like themselves.' It allowed the lot of them to be among the worst of humanity and rewarded them with all kinds of perks. The new system ended their return [1]permanently. Either you mended your ways, or the system ended your days. Crime under the old system was encouraged. Close examination of the old Justice System exposed there was a sanguine love affair between crime and the justice system. The changes were designed to eliminate crime. Instead of prison those found guilty of crimes were sent to Hospitals. For a cost of the equivalent of five thousand dollars they were decapitated for rape, or child molestation. Murderers were fed to starving piranhas. Removal of parts of the body was the punishment for lesser crimes. Liars' tongues were cut out and fed to the rats. There were no attorneys to wheedle a deal or find a flaw in the presentation of the situation. Psychologist and Psychiatrist had no arena in which to pontificate the remissions of criminal's parents, or anything else. Man had grown up and demanded all accept responsibility for the choices they made. Either you joined the team or you were not invited to remain in The Game.

Marijuana was decriminalized for medicinal *use;* it had proven to be of medical value. There existed more information that presented Marijuana as an aide to peaceful coexistence than was the case for alcohol. Alcohol proved to contribute to man's higher nature to be harmonious, congenial, and responsible. It stood in the way of peace, harmony, and human unification. Its nature is to make humans aggressive. It should've remained a criminal act to produce it. Many lives were lost due to its availability. Not the case for Marijuana. It was quite the opposite. The data on that did not lie.

The money spent on him was well spent. Open or closed He found prison a thing He could do without. He cost Tax Payers at least

$59,000 a year to keep Him clean, fed, medicated, and sheltered. He had been imprisoned by circumstance. It became clear to Him early in life preying upon people had negative consequences. However, the existing consequences did not deter criminal activity. Over the years it was increasing. The need for more prisons proved that fact to be true and accurate. No matter how you looked at it the old system was a huge waste of money and resources as well. Later He found criminal behavior was insane and generally uncorrectable. It had no bearing on what is Real or what is True. He understood committing crimes wouldn't be to his benefit. Yet, He committed a felony at age seventeen. He got away with it. How He got away with it was a miracle. Social practices that were deviant and despicable brought Him to the door of crime. Later, at age twenty-nine He was convicted of involuntary manslaughter. The crime carried a sentence of two to five years and eligibility for parole after eighteen months. He got into a couple of skirmishes and wound up doing the whole sentence. He was now thirty-four and a significant part of his life had been spent behind bars. As a young man He began creating rugs and carpets as a hobby. In prison he continued his hobby and had developed retail outlets to sell his rugs and carpets on consignment. Now He had to focus on expanding His operation.

Unconsciously He nervously fidgeted with the pages of the Manuel as His eyes took in the scenery. The bus went through some potholes in the highway and He was jostled about. The jostling about brought him back into the bus and His eyes came to rest on the manila envelope that accompanied the Manuel, He received. Mechanically, He opened the envelope and removed the contents. To His surprise the envelope contained a log of His prison history, among other things. He counted the pages over and over, saying all the while, "What a waste of time." One silly mistake had cost Him five valuable years of His life.

Although, it had been noised about throughout the prison system all prisons would be closed by the end of the year, no one believed it.

They said, "It could not be done." They were wrong. The prison idea was a waste of taxpayer money.

How could a system contrived on deception and fraud miss its mark by such a varying degree? The Templars, Elite and Illuminati had so miscalculated the step-by-step procedure that it left it wide open for Visionaries to circumvent their New World Order plan without any violence whatsoever. Both the Elite and the Illuminati under estimated the intelligence of the masses. The blinders were off and the people were seeing the ruse for what it was. They did not like what they saw. They saw the human suffering of the many caused by the insensitive few.

It was a mistake to depend on Capitalism and Democracy as the manipulation factors. The people had grown weary under its sledgehammer effect. Underneath the veneer of Capitalism laid the truth of it being a Sophisticated Form of Slavery. Under the veneer of Democracy laid the truth of it serving the sociopathic, greedy and self-indulgent. It was complicated yet simple and very difficult to see it for what it really was. Once discovered the day of its doom was at hand. It was forever outlawed. A major component of the guise in seeing Capitalism as slavery was, they kept proclaiming a slogan, "The land of the free and home of the Brave." Now, that brainwash was ineffective.

The world as He had known it no longer existed. He was going to fend for himself in a world where Crime no longer held an acceptable place. He was convinced a man who knew himself would have no problem earning the right and privilege of being alive.

God, Almighty, provides birds, elephants, and all of creation with what it requires to sustain itself. Man knowing himself is welcome to HIS guidance. Tragic things happen when Man convinces himself he must take things in his own hands. He becomes insane. He denies the existence of a Creator. That makes him insane. His insanity makes him less than Man. He is a beast. He robs, wars, lies,

Explores, rapes, molests, and tries to fashion a life which he deems desirable. At that self appointed position, he is mad. Man becomes a destroyer of the Real. Yet, prison was not the proper place for the mad men.

The Prison He was held in was the last to close. Over an eleven-year span the Prisons were closed and the inmates processed, for four years, before their release into society. They received a Manuel of fifty pages. Each page read the same. "Behave or be history!"

Before release each inmate underwent exit processing. It was structured to orient the inmates how the new system worked. The training or educating was redundant and intense. Instruction was ample with its main focus on personal accountability. Every effort was made to insure and assure each inmate would have a complete understanding of past criminal behavior as totally unacceptable. In the new system it would not be treated with anything but disdain and simple detachment; felonious acts would find no listening ear. The training was continuous in all Prisons over the eleven years span; granting those who were having difficulties assimilating as much time as reasonable to make the adjustments. Those inmates on Death Row met their fate in the first two years of the reconstruction. There was an out-and-out war on human insanity. It was mouthed that some of them may have been innocent; such is the nature of war. The Visionaries were aware of that possibility. In any war there is always the possibility innocent people will be victimized. The war on crime warranted no exclusions. Recalcitrance was not an option. Those who resorted to resistance were transferred to facilities that had the later closing dates. Those who caught on to the changes quickly were released sooner. Over the eleven-year span every man or woman who was a guest of State or Federal Institutions was thoroughly trained and reoriented to enter the main stream as a productive individual. Comply was the mandate and the only option. Capitalism had spawned a bastard child, "earning a living." It was replaced with a Parented child, "earning the right to be alive."

The instruction and training delved deeply into why previous systems met their demises.

Simply stated they lacked 'Truth.' Primarily, they were corrupt and biased. They were founded on the divide and conquer principle. In presentation, the 'melting pot' offered opportunities for all. The reality of it was all together different. It became the 'separation pot.' In presentation the system featured 'freedom, unity, and opportunity for better tomorrows. It pledged one thing and fostered another. Underneath its banner of red, white, and blue, it unfurled a dogma as black and obscure as ever was concocted. Sequestered amidst its presentation was the wedge of competition. Get the people competing with one another and they will be unable to see the real terrorist or enemy. It's sleight of hand Black Magic. It pitted the people against one another so they were blinded to the trick that was being played on them by the miscreant Templars, Bilderberg group, Masons, Shriners, Elite, Illuminati, and Skull Bones, Eastern Stars, plus other secret groups.

Having to compete with one another for everything did not unify the people. It secured separation. It created a vile climate of Hell. The working and productive people functioned in total bondage. They labored under the assumption that having a bunch of toys was a sign of something good. The people were taxed at uncanny rates. They slaved under the pretext of free enterprise and competition as a healthy social environment; it had the working and productive public sponsoring, securing, and funding their own bondage. Their labor and their money were financing it all. Simply stated, the people financed the Government and the Government ran the world for the ruling classes. Those who find themselves as advocates of this practice are insane. Those who abhor this practice are sane.

In exacting control of humans and their affairs at large levels of efficiency, money and miss education play key roles. When a group had money, money flowed to them. On the other hand, when a group has control of the minds of people, the people put money in their hands, with regularity. Through miss education people can be conditioned to support a dysfunctional Governing body. They can be coerced to pay taxes as a normal and an admirable duty.

Miss education has many a crooked face. The system had proven itself devious beyond imagination by controlling both, money and miss education. Using, numbers and images on paper the Templars eventually established a World Banking system. This achievement established the Monetary System as ruler of the entire world. It gave value to things that had no value, i.e. gold and diamonds. However, it lacked certain real things, morality, integrity, and understanding. Time would eventually dissolve the attempted unification of false and true. There are Universal Principles that defy the distorted rules of humans or human impersonators. As it grew it needed more-and-more money. Eventually it out grew its supply of money. When the money ran out miss education was useless. Greed, Corruption, and Lust, which are forms of extreme ignorance, brought it all down. Funding dysfunctional institutions similar to Its Justice System and Prison system were huge contributory factors in the crumbling of the old system.

A shortage of money to run it killed it. The money to run the system came from the people, in Taxation. In time the people were so unnecessarily taxed that they were paying tax on tax. Approximately eleven percent of the people were connected to and benefited from the system, with .01% of the world population attempting to successfully control it. It was the eighty-nine percent that were not connected who revolted. Mr. and Mrs. Tax Payer had no other option than face the reality of their being dupes for the Lazy Organizers of the system.

Many a hard-core criminal broke into blustering tears as they came face to face with the fact they were as much victims of the insanity as their victims. Crime funneled egregious sums of money into the economy. The justice system depended on the Criminals. The Criminals were their clients. Without clients the criminal justice system would be out of business. Money that time revealed was miss-spent served to perpetuate the problem of miscreant behavior, rather than remediate it; Law Enforcement, Probation Departments, Psychologists, Criminal Justices Courts, Psychiatrists, insurance agencies, home security systems, night watch men, armed guards, and guard dogs were necessary. These components symbolizing Social Order and others were dependent upon the perpetuation of Crime. When Crime went away so did they.

Imperialism, Capitalism, Colonialism, and Slavery are the most parasitic conditions humans can be forced to live under. Under the structure of the above-mentioned parasites, those in control made the rules. It was criminal. In America crime was so good to criminals, Europeans were seeking citizenship in America in droves.

The Rich, the Oppressive, and the Royal tried to use the tricks of Treason and Sedition to quell the dismantling of the New Way of Life. Their efforts met with frustration and disappointment, only. There were no demonstrations, no protests, and no civil unrest. There was no leader. Then, came a day that eighty-nine percent of the people refused to go to the job. No way could they lock up eighty-nine percent of the population. The people realized they could get along much better without the rich. There was no person to identify and charge as the leader of an insurrection. Collectively eighty-nine of the people had concluded the old way had to go. The Rich and Oppressive had no recourse but to acquiesce and yield to the wheel of time. Some of the rich believed they would regain the power in time. The less optimistic killed themselves and their families. Only a hand full of them was skilled at anything besides being stingy. Most only had a talent for oppressing. It boiled down to, they were useless. Their dirt and filth was uncovered; it lay quivering and spastic in the aura of Truth. Their rein had proven beyond doubt to be fraudulent. Time had made possible the over throw of repressive groups forever. The duping had seen its day at the Fair.

How were they duped? This was covered thoroughly as reform was explained every year of the four-year preparation transition to a system of self-government. Primarily, The justice system exploited them. Second, the super rich exploited them, and lastly, they lost their opportunity to be self-reliant. That was the most egregious of all the exploitations.

The justice system exploited them by using them as a means to create an officiously opulent way of life for those who constituted its component parts. It became a business all its own. Its clients were the gambit of Criminals it processed, most often over-and-over again. The system was operated with the intent of sustaining a growing Criminal population. Its beneficiaries were its constituents composed of judges, lawyers, law schools, psychologists, psychiatrists, parole boards, probation officer, Prisons, Prison Suppliers, Law enforcement officers, insurance companies, private security officers, and more. These entities were dependent upon the perpetuation of crime. It was bandy-boxed around closing the Prisons would cause the Economy to collapse. Without it they were sure to lose their high-lifestyles. The relationship between the Criminal and the Justice System was absolute symbiosis. They were partners.

The two were locked in union while proclaiming, overtly, different aims and objectives. The criminal was parasitically attacking the taxpayer by various discordant acts. The Criminal Justice System was parasitically attacking the Tax Payer by portending or presenting itself as the Tax Payers friend and companion in reducing or eliminating crime. It was a relationship that required simple deduction to determine the taxpayer was getting hammered from both sides. The taxpayer played into it by being gullible. Piercing the well-shrouded veneer was no easy task. The subtly of its application and institutionalization was considered as not only real, but also the normal state of things.

The super rich received huge sums of money for building "Correctional Institutions." These, public funded, institutions did everything but correct. The people provided the finances for supplying the correctional institutions with beds, machines, tools, stoves, food, linens, uniforms, handcuffs, chains, and were tendered very large insurance premiums to cover hazards, insurrections, and natural disasters. These correctional institutions did anything but solve the problem. They were cesspools of depravity. Homosexuality was ramped. The ministers and governing bodies turned their heads and permitted it, so they sanctioned it. Increased learning in crime was the order of the day. Gangs were formed and hostility was fed toward the taxpayer. Religious beliefs were perverted beyond limits. The "Bible" strictly prohibits homosexuality. The Judicial System approved of it by doing nothing to stop it. Some in the field of Psychiatry even defended it as normal human behavior. This might be the case at the lowest of the lower levels of human consciousness and development. Societies do not need institutions that foster this type of normalcy.

Worst of all things the Old System had to accept was the amount of money Crime contributed to the Economy. The amount of money generated by the perpetuation of crime was staggering. Removing crime would by itself demolish the system. That was a lie. The money funding the Criminal Justice system was to be used to remedy the inadequacy of quality housing for the people. For the first time in the History of America people realized they were providing free food, clothing, medical, and shelter for the wrong people, the criminals. It was backwards and the people had been miss educated to believe it was as it should be. The means to do this had always been at hand.

The connection between crime and the super rich was a thing of fanciful romance. The laws were structured by the Rich to make many things legal that were illegal and harmful. Alcohol is an Addictive beverage. It was legal. Drunks kill people. The Rich made it legal to kill in War. Killing human beings outside of war was illegal.

Legal was determined by the rich who had might, but who were not necessarily right in consciousness or common sociability. Man was buying stones, gold, and silver and believing it had value. They were being sold the idea of destroying the environment as somehow related to human Advancement. Humans were being sold a daily dose of forced reality without notification or clarification.

Wholesale robbery was center stage as Mr. and Mrs. Tax Payer were lulled into believing they were free and getting something for their money. All the while they were being robbed and mostly enslaved by not knowing who they were. They were being exploited.

The conditioning was so well scripted; so deep, and so well hidden from conscious awareness that Mr. and Mrs. Tax Payer were thoroughly convinced they had the best of all worlds.

Through exposing compromised religious beliefs, academic anesthetization, and the promise of a future offering total indolence they had become deaf, dumb and blind to reality and willfully submitted to forms of function in the place of Reality. Thereby consigning them all together into a ridiculous condition of self-monitoring exploitation. They were puppets on a string.

Mr. and Mrs. Tax Payer had bought the program of War as a thing of duty. They pledged allegiance to a symbol and sent their children off to warring with nobility in their bosoms. This level of Insanity was the norm. A ravaged social group had lost its collective mind.

That had all been changed and the mission was clear and purpose was more defined and conceivable and an attainable success was achievable. The obstructions to the "Path" were no longer formidable adversaries. Now they were more neutralized than ever before. Self-Mastery was the companion to seek. With the dawning of self-awareness had come a bastion of light and insight that was Herculean and in self-propelling in thrust. At last there was a reason for living. All things animate and inanimate had purpose and destination. The relationship between all things seen and unseen was congruently intertwined as self and useful extensions or supports in development of Self.

During the eleven-year reconstruction period there were many struggles and much pain. The Super Rich were ready to do battle to maintain their feet upon the Tax Payers' necks in the name of good. The pleas of the oppressed were unwarranted and they were unwilling to concede they had been found out. It did not matter. The people had had it.

At long last Mr. and Mrs. Taxpayer discovered they had nothing to lose and everything to gain by abandoning the System. It was clear the System was a wayward child and at best a Beast.

The bus slowed to a stop at the Station, and he got off. His destination was within waling distance. The sky was clear and he felt lethargic so walked. It did him good to walk. Being cramped in the close quarters of the bus had made him stiff. As he walked He examined the contents of the envelope. One of the papers had an Address on it. Here would be His habitat until He could provide better for Himself. He had no probation officer to report to. There would be no exams for drug use. He had to either swim or drown. The period of social stupidity was over and done. It was a brand new day and He could smell it in the air. It was clean and fresh. For the first time in His life He tasted experienced no fear, and He like it.

Chapter

2

THIS IS SERIOUS

He RANG THE DOORBELL and a man responded. The man saw the envelope at a glance and told him to come in. He followed the man to a sitting room where the man went behind a modest desk and motioned him to have a seat. The man extended his hand and said, "Call me Turk. He gave Turk the envelope and said, "It's nice to meet you." Turk nodded acknowledgement and searched through the packet removing the papers he needed.

He sat there for a few moments tapping on the desk and finally broke the awkward silence with, "Do you have any questions?" He answered, "Yep." Turk said, "Shoot." "What kind of place is this?" He said, "It is a starter dwelling. You need some time and get acquainted with the materials in the envelope before you venture out in search of your place in this system."

Saying follow me Turk got up and stepped to the door. He followed. They reached the end of the hall and Turk opened the door. He stepped back and politely nodded for Him to enter. He did. Turk closed the door behind him and all He could hear was Turks fading footsteps echoing down the hall.

He was surprised at His surroundings. It was comfortable for one person. It was furnished with a 39 inch wall Visio monitor, a double bed, oversized lazy boy chair, small kitchen, shower and toilet facilities, closet, dresser, refrigerator, kitchen table and two kitchen chairs, a desk and computer with printer, and a self contained heat and air conditioning unit. Inside the closet was a linen closet with clean linens and towels. It had two windows on the South side and one on the East side. He sat His valise on the floor, sprawled in the oversize chair and closed His eyes. His thoughts wandered. Eventually, the reason for the drastic changes in social development became vividly clear.

In the past the Tax Payers were paying to sustain mediocre living conditions in public housing. That was scrapped. It demeaned people and was unacceptable. To a great extent it was a major part of the problem of crime. Now everyone had improved standards of living. The citizens were receiving the best of socialized health care. Safety was not an issue. They exhibited pride and high moral character. Most importantly Mr., and Mrs. Tax Payer were no longer impoverished in human entitlements.

It must have been twenty-four years ago that the first serious movement began to secure health benefits for all people in the country as human entitlement. Funds were available to provide health care for convicts, elected officials, the ruling class, and the elite. The postulate was everyone inhabiting and comprising the populous of a region was entitled to Universal Health Care. Medical and health care were unified under the umbrella of human entitlement accorded each individual as a share of the common wealth of the land and the World Community. It took fifteen years for the established medical institutions to find in favor the truth of this postulate. The elite fought the change by using the National Guard and Police to put down, what they attempted to term insurrection.

In the past people were beaten and mutilated to maintain the status quo. This time the people did not show up to demonstrate. Employers laid people-off, fired people and bullied people with threats and intimidation. Secret and covert organizations used scare tactics to discourage people from uniting towards obtaining health care. Nothing worked to dismantle the trust of the movement to guaranty each person health care. Visions of children being attacked by dogs and women beaten were conjured up as the journey out of yesterday continued.

People were randomly beaten in attempts to insight the people to riot. These antics served to show the displeasure the Rich were experiencing in the struggle to keep things as they were, only. He began to sweat and toss-and-turn as the anguish of the peoples suffering and enslavement filled the room. His breathing was labored for a moment. That time had come and gone.

The World frowned upon the past conduct of the Rich and Royal. After much suffering and abuse the people came to solidarity and concluded the best way to render a Cobra or Rattlesnake harmless was not to defang it, but to neutralize it. En masse they stopped buying certain products vital to the status as well as the living styles of the Elite. In tandem boycotting certain products coupled with the work stoppage was effective. As the Elite found themselves selling fewer and fewer products to the Mr. and Mrs. Tax Payer the sweet dreams of the rich and elite became distasteful nightmares. The Elite have but one talent, making money. It is a talent the world could do very well without. Greed showed its treacherous nature and dug its teeth into the parlors of their mansions. So distraught were they that the set about forming committees to revisit the idea of human entitlement. They had to agree that they had no more right to the abundance of the world than anybody else. What's more they had to accept the misery facing them was of their own doing. They had contrived ways to garner unfair shares of the wealth of the world and now were paying the tab. It hurt. In the past they had been the hammers. Now they were being the nails. They had structured laws and regulations that offended Universal Principles and time demanded its due.

The construction and design of the system was so diabolical and satanic no one could've conceived of it being a false reality and implicitly Witch Craft of the most bestial kind. So over burdened with securing basic entitlements was Man that he had no time to question his circumstances. The criminal Justice System was so structured with a complex methodology that what was just and fair was treated as unjust and unfair. This made it impossible for people to come by basic entitlements. It was illegal to wound a burglar or intruder in your own home, in California. The intruder may sue a person defending themselves against an intruder, in their home. It was legal for a burglar to sue the occupants of any home who assaulted him in the process of committing a criminal act against the occupants. This is one example of the biased structure of the old System.

None of the people's possessions were safe from natural disaster. People were oriented to maintain living quarters that were mostly opulent and costly to rebuild. The idea of a home had mushroomed into a very complicated burdensome chore requiring insurance that the insurance companies were reluctant to honor. When the insurance companies did pay up they raised the clients premiums. Simple and modest living quarters were frowned upon and the practicality of what a home was, negated by bigger-and better as the order of the day. The people had become lost in a maze of acquiring more space than they needed. Along with this aberration came the need for more to be made secure. Mr. and Mrs. tax payer had to bring in more money to pay for less or at best the same. What one parent provided before now required two parents. Roles were less defined and people were confused as to what they were supposed to do as males and females. The result was the beginning of the destruction of the nuclear family. The extended family had already gone by the wayside. It led to accepting of single family and homosexual family as okay.

Meanwhile, people were being evicted by land lords and lending institutions with reckless abandon. Under the prevailing system of Witch Craft Mr. and Mrs. Tax Payer plus children and seniors were dislodged from their living quarters and tossed in the streets as unwanted discards. The fabricators of that demonic system had assumed the right to hold hostage the ill begotten land and harness Mr. and Mrs. Tax Payer with indebtedness for human entitlements. In this respect primitive and savage cultures were more advanced than the fashioners of the new world. The practice of making people homeless for any reason is beyond barbaric, savage, and inhumane. One man can make a difference.

A hard workingman lost his job. Due to the current recession his boss had to go out of business. The man's unemployment benefits were nowhere near what he required to just stay a float. So, after six months he had begun to default on his mortgage. Next, his unemployment benefits ran out. Searching here, there, and everywhere he was unable to find relief from his dilemma. Eventually the bank foreclosed and he was notified of impending eviction.

Came the day of his eviction and the Sheriff arrived. This event marked the beginning of the collapse of the old system of providing shelter. To the sheriff's surprise the home was vacant. All the families' furniture, tools, and miscellaneous items were heaped in the street. They were burnt to a crisp. Everything had been destroyed and rendered useless. It was all reduced to ash and trash. The street was impassable and a News Crew just happened to be in the area to capture the incident. It made the evening news, from that moment on others adapted the practice and the Cities were overwhelmed with the fall out from evicting people.

The Cities had no provisions for storage of the tons of household goods that were being incinerated in the middle of City Streets, as a result of evictions. Land Fills were in short supply. Planned Obsolescence had seen to that and, the inclination towards a 'throw-away-society together made it impossible to support the practice of eviction. Nor did the Cities have facilities to incarcerate the evictees or fine them for littering. To fine them would be a waste of time. Plus it would be necessary to find them to fine them. Since they were evicted they had neither home nor address. How much sense does it make to fine someone who you are unable to find? They were homeless. Once evicted, they could not be found. The collective tenor of the people's actions wrenched the power from the Mortgage Goliaths and laid the foundation for change.

Thus, it was determined decent housing was a human entitlement and not a societal privilege.

No system that obtains its right through might is worthy of either accolades, or cooperation from its citizens. Cooperation and respect are things that must be earned in all areas of life. Compliance obtained by brainwash and indoctrination wilts and dries and turns to dust. Oppression in time blows the dust away with the oscillating wind of Truth.

Brainwashed people will submit to nonsense. How else could people be brought to suffer paying a person for shelter? How else could a person be in accord with buying something he can neither move, nor claim constant use of unless the Taxes are paid? How can people pay three times the purchase price of a home to an industry that is in a constant state of financial ruin, unless they are brainwashed or under a negative spell? The Mortgage and Banking institutions were consistently having financial problems. Of course Mr. and Mrs. Tax Payer had to consistently bail them out. Once they were back on their feet, they in turn would put Mr. and Mrs. Tax Payer on the street, in the event they were unable to pay the mortgage. It took seventeen years of struggle to right this travesty. The total situation was bazaar. It was only tenable due to orientation to "normal" life and miss education. It was promulgated by the deceptive fabricators of a false reality, constructed for the sole benefit of master witches and warlocks. Ironically it was all done under a dark cloud of good.

Time is the great equalizer. Time has the capacity to bring about change without a leader. When time intervenes there is no way to alter its thrust or stop its momentum. In time the people began to awaken to some simple facts and truths. Among them was this truth, "Anytime a person has something and someone else can legally taken it away, it was never theirs. In reality they were simply lulled into a deluded state of compliance to false reality. The fear of loss made them comply. All the while the objects they thought they had possession of were things by which they were being manipulated and not for their good. The Coup de Gras was the job.

The job was the most dishonest component of the deception. It constituted an advanced, subtle, but most efficient title for the social position of the new slaves. Under its implementation the company store had dominion and humans were disposable. A person had to have a job in order to get money. Without money a person was unable to obtain anything. The warlocks controlled who and how money was circulated.

Job was a fitting nomenclature coined by the skillful lexicographers for a subservient role. Its definition intertwined with work in a muddled way. The actual definition of JOB is, "Debasing oneself to others to facilitate the others in creating and hopefully maintaining luxurious life-styles for themselves. In exchange the others were issued a paycheck for their labors. Usually the paycheck provided the laborers just enough money to get back to the job Monday morning.

Money afforded the perpetrators of the Witch Craft a means to control who had and who went lacking. It was a system of using numbers on pieces of paper that were, in reality, valueless. Money cannot reproduce itself, which makes it false. It isn't real. The veil of neo slavery was thick and engulfed all people who had jobs. What had eventually emerged was, 'an everybody goes when the wagon comes' form of slavery. No one who generated under several billions of dollars per year was immune to the ravages of colonization, greed, and human exploitation. People were being black mailed for bare necessities. Now, they had come full circle and awakened to the reality of their not being free at all.

Imperialism is the worst of the worst kind of slavery. It is extreme in socially deviant oppression and devised by depraved and misanthropic kinds of people. It is so very subtle, most people had no idea they were slaves struggling under the ravages of Imperialism. Its sophistication is unparalleled. So is its violence.

Its use had required yet another task delegated to the programmers or teachers. They coined a nonsense phrase and gave it life, **"Earning a living."** The phrase implies a direct and unflappable link between living and earning money. Earning a living can't be done. It implies should a person become ill there would be no need for a Doctor. All the person would have to do is earn more money. There is no truth in the words **"Earn a living."** Therefore, the saying is false.

Further, no other life form required money to live. *It is impossible to earn a living. One may earn the right to be alive by being upstanding and a compliment to life.* That is doable. It is possible to earn money and create a life-style. The fact is, life style and money are directly related in social orders of Capitalism, Imperialism, and Slavery. The use of money hides the oppression covertly masked by the programmed messages featured in the documents of declaration of intent. The actual state and condition of Things coinciding with daily implementation to the declarations did not exist. Mr. and Mrs. Voter were convinced they were not only free, but also had some say in the events, and coming and goings of their lives. They were programmed and educated to hand rap and visit these miseries on their children and future generations as their legacy.

However, the spell was broken by the long and anguished suffering that Mr. and Mrs. Tax Payer had endured. As if by some miraculous bond of unification most of the groups came to the same conclusion, the Slave Masters had to go. The eras of divide and conquer lay smoldering as heaps of ashes devoid of power. When the smoke cleared all but a few admitted they all had the same problem and were suffering under the same oppression. A method evolved that would sever those ends. Collectively they stopped drinking alcoholic beverages, buying cars, paying property taxes, buying gasoline, and smoking cigarettes.

A day came day when most of the people refused to go to the Jobs. It started with a few people. As the word got out that the wars against oppression were under way more people just stayed at home.

This was the dawning of the reality of, the people as the driving force of their own suppression and subjugation. The power had been in their hands all along. The Witch Craft Masters had convinced the people they had no power. Everything gradually stopped. Not one single thing was in operation. Even the hospitals were closed. After two weeks some people died. Such is the case of war. People die in war. The difference in this war was nobody was killed. In this regard the war was different, people died, but there was no killing. They died from hunger, and over exposure to the elements. Then a familiar sound He had not heard for five years got His attention, and He opened His eyes.

The August rain pelting the windows on the South side of His living quarters, in blustery torpidity, summoned Him from the reverie. He rubbed his eyes and yawned as one aroused from a deep sleep. He stood, stretched and headed toward the refrigerator. It was night and the light from the refrigerator shot out of the open door with blinding force. It was well stocked with basic food. The restructuring mended many fences. He made a ham sandwich on whole wheat bread, with roman lettuce, and sliced tomatoes, with mayonnaise, and can of malt beer. Poverty was a thing of the past. People no longer feared starving, and War had been totally eradicated. The focus of the holy Jihad was where it had finally found fulfillment, self-mastery.

Under the new system everyone was provided with the basics food, clothing, safety against crime, medical, and shelter. It was regarded as an International Crime to withhold these basics by any means or contrivance. The state of desperation that was the main stay of Imperialism, Monarchism, and Slavery in its many deceitful disguises was neutralized. The outcome was a joy to be a part of. It eliminated crimes involving persons and property, and insured safety. Closing the prisons had been a stroke of genius. Under the new system crimes against people were out of the question. Anyone found guilty of a crime against a person was executed within two days. Evidence or two witnesses determined guilt. There were no lawyers, no appeals, and no excuses for crimes involving harm to others persons. A state of safety permeated the climate of the world. Through studies conducted over forty years it had been concluded, denial of basics or difficulty on obtaining basics was the major factor in criminal acts, generally.

War was outlawed and forbidden. A group of highly trained international assassins was formed and maintained for the sole purpose of hunting down and assassinating any, and all War Mongering Maniacs, throughout the World. Historically war had proven itself to be lacking in its validity to continue financing it. The beneficiaries' of war were the Rabble who sold bullets, bandages, and reconstruction supplies. Further, the Rabble who profited financially from war was the only beneficiaries of the carnage. The greater good was accepted as that which was most fulfilling in content to allow people to prepare to meet their Creator. Self-development was the means by which this had been deemed possible. Education featured Self-Mastery as its major concern.

In a moment of rationality people became acutely aware of their mortality. In that flash of awakening the Throne of England came crashing down. Royalty was the bastion of Imperialism. Royalty represents the epitome of opulence and self-indulgence. Historically the explorers ventured forth to take the resources of others. Historically the Royal families financed theses expeditions destroying healthy and vibrant cultures. When the explorers met with resistance against colonization, the Royal Thrones declared war on the resistors. The authority for theses intrusions into the lives of others was might, not right. Their only contributions to living were self-indulgence, oppression, and taking in the name of good. The conquered people had their own religions. Albeit it their religions were not formal. Their Religions were more of a disciplined way of life than Rituals and Ceremonies. Although they had a loving reverence for the Deity they worshipped and loved the Deity more than feared IT.

The Imperialists turned the tables on Mr. and Mrs. Tax Payer; they programmed them to fear death. Worst than that through

Organized Religion, they programmed Slaves, Mr. and Mrs. Taxpayer to fear God rather than love HIM. Religion was used to compel people to do whatever they could do to live as long as possible. Possessions and Matter became more important and relative to existence than practicing peaceful co-existence, being, and Self-Mastery. They had been programmed to fear that which was unavoidable, existing life. They had become so disjointed from the Real that they were strangers to the present and fearful of the future. They were empty shells programmed to cut one another's throats and pray to Jesus Christ for forgiveness. Organized Religion held the promise of lighting the way in its right hand, and pointed the way to one of the darkest periods in the history of man with its left hand. Imperialism had won the day. To its dismay, it had not won out over Time. All falsehood must and will dwindle and fall with the passing of Time. The Crowns and ceremonies of oppressions lay writhing in the yellow slim of human defilement. Royalty had no talents apart from laziness and conniving; they were helpless in their new role. They were useless. Such was the case with the demise of Imperialism.

People performed task to contribute meaningfully to their culture and to socially self-develop. There were no such things as jobs. There was work. People were able to see themselves in their contributions toward maintaining vigorous Cultures.

Competition had moved center stage in the reconstructed world. Competing with others for self-validation was recognized as the lower end of competition. It was not shunned, nor was it discouraged. Most assuredly, it was neither encouraged nor promoted. The ideas of determining who they were or what their status was because they could perform a task better than someone else put a person in a state of negative self identity dependence. It created a state where one had to be more at the expense of another being less. That comprised a negative dependency state. The higher end had been identified as competing with oneself in self-development as a state of positive dependency and natural in man's self-development. Purpose had mounted to self-projection through excellence in being and performing. No matter what people did they had as goals improving performance. The sanguine idea that unless some outward force drove a person, they would become torpid had proven itself to be a tool of manipulation, only. It was destitute of truth.

He had mastered the skills of carpet weaving during the last four years of His imprisonment. Each inmate was thoroughly trained to produce something by which he could engage in barter. The acquired and refined refinement of talents constituted the individuals contribution to his community or nation. He could engage in barter to obtain discretionary credits. The acquired refinement of talents constituted the individuals contribution to his community or nation. No man had to earn a living as touted by Capitalism. Under the new System of Human Nationalism everybody had to **earn the right to be alive**. All trade was conducted by barter. Selling for tokens, money, conk shells or whatever was obsolete. Education included the why's of this change to barter and the necessity for improvement in social amalgamation.

The Committee unanimously agreed Money as a means of exchange for goods or labor had to be discontinued. It was assigned a value by an agency in Switzerland. The insult was, it acted as an intermediary or go between to collect a fee for mankind on most transactions. These fees were justified as necessary to make things better for Man. It was a rank lie. History, as unreliable as it is shows clearly just the opposite is the case. The committee had no trouble finding evidence of the fact that money was an ill conceived plot to gain unfair advantages, and it was money's nature to offer no more than that to the life experience.

Primarily, barter eliminates middlemen. The people involved in transactions must be able to determine the value of items offered for transfer from one to the other. The negotiation between the two people assures both of them of their ability to make equitable exchanges. Barter is even more useful in human interactions than Money, because it establishes self-reliance. Beyond that the people involved in the transaction know best the value of the items involved in the trade to them. Most importantly, the barter system neutralizes greed. It is impossible to hoard in the system of barter, without dire consequences to the hoarder. Usually the bartered items are perishables. What makes the barter system more equitable is the fact that it assists in maintaining social parity.

No man's work is more important to a social system than any others. Each man's contributions to his community is of equal valuable to the next and must equate to decent returns. An efficient System functions best are honoring each person's contribution equally. The Stipend system makes this possible. Under the Stipend Barter system a man has the opportunity to determine his worth by his own productiveness. His fate and destiny is in his hands and his Creators. Under the monetary system the qualified usually carry the weight of the unproductive staff. It's called many names, "The good old boys club, the click, the klatch, the in crowd," and many more pseudonyms." The use of money supports the premise of Capitalism as an ideal system. That is true in the sense of it is ideal for the lazy, shiftless, and conniving among the living. Money afforded the lazy an opulent life-style. Non-productive people got to ride the train of life without contributing anything worthwhile.

In manufacturing everything they produce results in harm to the environment and eventually becomes trash.

Those who profited most from Capitalism were the parasitic, the stingy, and the lazy. With the appearance of the Stipend Barter system the above had no place. They were required to live on the fruits of their labors. Being parasites, they had acquired no skills. They were denied the accumulation of credits.

The transition from the monetary system to the Stipend Barter system took eight years. After which time the means of exchange for goods or labor was barter. The Stipend allowed all people to have discretionary and disposable credits.

Throughout the ages money had been the blackened face of Tyranny and Government had been its twisted and decrepit body. Tyranny had met an opponent of enormity comparable to render it powerless and inert. Eighty-nine percent of the people had made it discernibly clear; they would rather die than perpetuate the oppression and bondage, of the past, to future generations.

It was a matter for Time to settle and time was equal to the task. Subsequently, the dawn of a new beginning announced the resurgence of redefined Education, re-principled Religion, and reemphasis of Self-Mastery.

Chapter

3

EDUCATION AND RELIGION

IN THE OLD SYSTEM the function of education was two dimensional, "Control of the behavior of large numbers of people, and vocational preparation." That was far from education. It was outright wicked organized and uniquely structured Witch Craft. In General, people who lack self-control consistently plan on controlling others. These types typically practice forms of skillful Witch Craft.

Under the new system everybody had to attend high school classes or college classes three evenings per week. It was necessary to bring the people out of that darkness slowly and consistently. Reorienting people to what is real is no easy task. The circumstances required a different approach to educating the people. Education had a different purpose. Education had as its goal helping everyone develop in Self-Mastery. Know thy self first. Then, teach them how to live together successfully.

There was ample time for additional schooling, because under the new system everybody received a stipend. It was awarded as a human entitlement. Elders had concluded everyone would receive an equal potion of the Common Wealth without equivocation. The things He had learned in prison, about life, during His imprisonment would become further developed and discussed in more depth and relativity.

Education had advanced beyond cookie cutting, conditioned response manipulating, and slot preparation.

The next day he visited the neighborhood school. Under the old Education Policy and Practice the focus was on first, programming the slaves to accept their slavery as normal and a good thing thereby, securing the hold on neo-slavery. Second, on convincing the slaves the purpose for living was the acquisition of stuff. Lastly, the pursuit of pleasure, fame and fortune were the ultimate treasures of life. Later, that dogma proved to be brainwashing.

Securing a hold on the slaves was achieved by structuring a sustainable system, which guaranteed the slaves could have their minimal needs met by using money, only. To get the money the slaves had to do the bidding of the slave masters. In return the slaves gave the money back to the slave masters for the things the slaves were naturally entitled to. The slave masters had set up a system that positioned them as middlemen. Money allowed them to control everything and they determined who would get the lions' share of the loot. Ingeniously this took the freedom of life and happiness from the slaves. It made them docile and compliant to the devious demands of the slave masters.

Every aspect of the old education system highlighted this process as normal and real. The differences in living conditions of the slave masters and the slaves were swept under the rug. The slaves were regarded as unimportant and insignificant. There was an overabundance of them and it was easy to replace the fallen. The slaves were given colorful names such as the Working Class, the Consumer, the Guest, etc. They were lulled into an obscure reverie by the educational process.

Figurative decapitation of the slaves came easy as the slave masters ventured into divers methods of deluding the slaves. The slave masters heralded inventions. Each invention was ear marked to further entrap the slaves. As mice scurrying to be snared in traps the slaves came in hoards, droves, and colonies to take the bait. They surrounded themselves with stuff. The ultimate requital for the acquisition of stuff was fear. The slaves had to insure the stuff against loss or damage. Meaningless objects were assigned great value by the slave masters stones and metals. A stone is a stone. Items that had no real worth in them became things people would kill each other for, but were worthless as life's necessities. For life's purposes they were insignificant and gimmicks. With these trinkets they beckoned the slaves to pursue lives of self-indulgence.

Embedded richly in the old education system was the congeniality of pleasure. It was assiduously emphasized during and through the education processing that the main and primary substance or content of life's offerings was excessive living. It was touted as the ultimate measure of a life successfully lived. What a ruse!

No person ever took the material trappings acquired during a waste of a life span acquiring material objects along when they died. Fame and fortune are the pursuits of the badly misguided. The old educational system presented them as the ultimate achievements. Education was more of indoctrination than an efficient preparation for social development and self-realization. Education harped on excess and doing whatever could be done without consideration for how that attitude impacted upon everything else.

That attitude, regarding education, was totally subjective and completely dissociated from the reality of all that is being parts of a whole, the ONE. It avoided accountability and responsibility for human behaviors and established no relationship between proper actions and improper actions as assessed against results. Instead it happily concocted a mumble jumble legal system that worked best at doling out justifications for abominable and deplorable acts.

Upon being admitted to his first class He was surprised to find He was not the eldest person in the class. Half of the class was composed of older people. It was a History class. It was different and felt exciting. For the first time lessons in History were fashioned to contain solutions for past non-productive acts. Instead of fostering Patriotism i.e. who shot John, when, where, why and how. It examined what John was doing when he got shot, and sought to prevent John from doing that again. Each session they examined what was it that led man to lose self-control. Some of the classes examined what drove men to violate holy ordinances and decrees by God such as, "Thou shall not kill." They further examined why and how man became convinced God did not know what he was talking about when he spoke that commandment to Moses. It was exciting.

His excitement was not short lived. The students talked quietly among themselves as the clime in the room was set in that manner. All talking ceased when the guide entered the room. The guide greeted the students with, "Welcome to the first day of your proper development."

Mr. Anderson projected a holograph from his cell phone and began the session with a word "CHOICE."

He asked a student in the rear of the class, "Was war a natural occurrence, or is it a result of a kind of man's contrived choice?" The student rose to his feet and responded, "War will always be a matter of choice. It is unnecessary and benefits those who obtain control of the resources of others as well as those who profit from supplying materials for war, and those who profit from the reconstruction after the war."

The Guide smiled and said, "You sound like a tape recording! Either you are brainwashed or that is a speech you have had drummed into your conscious mind, by me." Mr. Anderson laughed at his own joke.

Then, he turned his attention away form the student and his eyes flashed across the entire student body as he spoke. "He is crazy, right? War is necessary in order for Progress to advance its cause?" His glance returned to the standing student and he said, "Your statement is candid. Can you support your position with fact?"

The student's name was Kip Kutupata. He frowned and said, "When we examine history we see the people have never been the beneficiaries of war. So why should they chose to fight? The resources of the people conquered insured the invaders improved life-styles, and at best, stability in misery for the people. It is there on the pages of history. As biased as History is, when read it is read with the eye of objectivity the records show it clearly."

"Please sit, Mr. Kutupata." He walked back and forth in front of the class tapping his holographic pen on his left index finger. He stopped and let out a sigh. Then he said, "How many of you agree with Mr. Kutupata?" "Show your agreement by raising your hands." The class size was forty, give or take one or two students. Of the students roughly thirty raised their hands in agreement. The Guide selected a young woman who hAD not raised her hand. He asked her to stand. Then he said, "Mrs. Hopkit, I am unclear about Mr. Kutupata's response to my question. Are you able to shed more light on the subject?"

She rose from her seat and began her response to the question. "War contains many choices and is most assuredly a matter of choice itself. I agree with that, but there is much more to it than that. Primary among the choices, contained in war, is the participation in it. When the young people stopped showing up to fight the wars, the Leaders stopped having them. The prime mover in welcoming that choice is being convinced a person has something to defend, or protect. Sadly many who return from wars in the past found they had nothing to protect.

Many who returned from war found they had no place in the very system they fought to protect. For years young people went to war believing valor could be found in patriotism and heroic deeds. Neither patriotism, nor heroism will establish anything of urgency in a man's life. These are words used as 'buttons' to manipulate young and unsuspecting people."

"They were brainwashed into believing they were serving country or nation and protecting something of value for themselves. The old education system incorporated History into the system to foster Patriotism. It turned out to be a bad choice predicated on bogus information. The choice was errant, because it neither benefited the people, nor the youth who went away to fight. Over time it was blatantly revealed they were merely defending the rights of the privileged. Examination of history revealed evidence, which refutes war being of benefit to participants. It was a bad choice. No matter what the promised expectation of the outcome of war fact is the rich got richer during and after war and the plight of the common people got worst or remained the same. It became painfully apparent; the common man would be no worst off regardless who won the war. Upon arriving at that conclusion, the young people decided it was a poor choice and no longer participated in it. Going to war reaped negligible benefits for the combatants."

"Thanks to research and the information highway the better choice concerning war was realized. There would be no more wars."

"Another choice is the choice to kill. Killing is always a choice. In verification of reality killing is the result of choice and not reality. Dying is inevitable. It is inescapable. At some unknown time and place every man must depart from life. That is reality. When the time comes death cannot be stayed. The choice to kill can be put off or disregarded. Killing is under the control of the individual. Dying is not under the control of Man. Killing is taking something that cannot be returned. Killing humans is always a choice. It is inexcusable. There is no justification for killing."

She went on, "In the past it was accepted that during war killing was okay. That too, was pure brainwash. The acceptance of that was one of the all times shrewdest, and dubious ploys ever played on man. There are no reasons why one man should kill another man, no matter who sanctions it. Man is free to kill anything but Man. During the dark period when man was instructed to kill man for the sake of Country, it was done with great efficiency but to the detriment of his species. Time, again, came to the rescue. It was discovered the common man had nothing to lose and nothing to gain from war. The greatest terrorist prevalent to his well being was the Capitalist, the Imperialists and other riffraff. They had engineered a scheme involving the use of money, numbers on paper or coin, that demanded the common man perform as they requested. Warring on other men was a major part of the scheme."

"This choice, to kill, was an indoctrinated choice. It was an insane choice. It is insanity to kill someone because you are told to do so. In application it was classic stimulus response technique. It was mechanical and the common man never knew he lacked self-control in this choice to kill. The common stimulus that was introduced, and proven successful was fear of loss, and the response triggered, kill and defend. It had become a forced choice. Nevertheless, it was a choice. It was very difficult to dismantle this type of conditioning. Ultimately, it was not a choice that was being made; it became a stimulus response in remission. In situations and circumstances of mass or group conditioning, at this level, it may be difficult to reverse the conditioning, but not impossible. Three agents were enlisted to reverse its affect and compulsion, Patience, Perseverance, and Time."

II was concluded war would no longer be a part of the human experience in problem solving. It was a choice and not a positive one."

She sat down and the Guide, Mr. Claude Anderson, bowed his head and spoke, as if talking to the floor, "Anybody have any question or additions to that?"

Hands flew up all around the classroom. He said, "Okay for the remainder of our time we will break up into groups of eight and discuss what the two speakers shared with us. Each group will meet independently to discuss and develop a position on Choices. At our session next week we will hear each groups' position on Choices. Select a spokesperson and be clear on key points, of your sharing, you have identified as questionable. Let's break for fifteen minutes."

After break Claude started a journey into Religion.

Religion no longer focused on fear and reprisal. It was approached as the initial step one must leap into before tackling any thing else in life. Some previous religious instructions featured God as the worker. The new approach to it sought to inspire Man to be agents for God and fulfill his will by submitting their wills to his. Theologians, ministers, and all religious scholars agreed no pure success could be attained until one had found union with God. That was the starting point of your beginning. It was taught birth was the beginning of your exit to a new beginning. Therefore, your every act must ensure you are preparing for your exit, since exiting is inescapable. Success then became defined as finding Union with God before exiting life.

This preparatory approach to Religion highlighted living in the manner of daily practice. It respected Religious basics, rituals, ceremonies, and incantations of the old school religious wise. However, its focus was on practicing humility, respect and care for all that exists.

Mr. Anderson led the students into a discussion of Organized and Formal Religion by asking, "Which of these two serves as a benefit to man Religion or Religiousness?" A hand shot up in the middle of the classroom. Mr. Anderson said, "Yes Tarrah?"

She replied, "In theory the two words are of equal relevance and import. However, in day-to-day operation and utility they are far apart. In the past pagan cultures forced rituals, sacrifices, festivals, and so on to intercede for the lack of spiritual content contained in the religious practices, as they lead no where. No matter how long one prayed, or did the rosary their status remained the same. They came no closer to God. The processes available to them were intended to hobble them and blind them into hopelessness. The subtly of it all was efficient enough to make them believe there was something wrong with them or their sacrifice, anything but the truth of their being deliberately misled. The tenets of the religious were simply designed to fill a void. To that end they were outstanding."

She continued, "The colonizers and imperialist were adepts at ministering to the black arts. They new repetitious rituals would lead the slaves only so far into the reality of the Journey. Detribalization of the Slaves adherence to their ceremonies and rituals insured the Colonizers the slaves would stagnate. Their spiritual growth and development was stymied. In maximum application Rituals offer the most benefit during the period of initiation. Those who realize the most benefit from the innovational rituals are those who are purest of heart and enwrapped in the cloak of burning passion for nearness to God. Even for the most advanced the progress in union was stultified. The rituals became the connection between the slave to man, only. Under the guise of religion and using religious books and artifacts they controlled the slaves, mostly with fear of Hell! The slaves had to be to their masters the opposite of what the slave masters were being to them. Those are some of the characteristics of the religious. The religious fear death. This fear was the most dynamic contrivance the colonizers imposed on the consciousness of the slaves. The slave would do anything to keep from dying. The Religious see Religion as a thing separate and apart from themselves. Those who have made the connection with God become Religion More than a Man."

As to Religion she said, "Religion is outside the control of men, warlocks, and or slave masters. Religion is the Path itself." She sat down as if she was a cloud of angelic energy. "When one has transcended in consciousness to be one with Religion, you have become the Path."

Seated, she continued, "The word Religion is a noun. Religion is a thing. It is the way of the properly behaved in life. Religious describes or is attributable to fundamental behaviors, actions, or more candidly actions leading to the acquisition of Religion. The word religious is an Adjective. An adjective describes a noun and its characteristics. A noun is the thing itself." Beginning there we can determine Religious may be initiations, rituals, books, hymns, paraphernalia, alters, ceremonies, etc. Religion on the other hand, is a self-disciplined way of life. As a thing, realized, it can only grow and become. At that point it ceases to be Religious and passively inactive. Once realized Religion takes on the form of the key active part of a person. It becomes a way of interacting with all things.

Then it becomes a discipline. In its evolving to a discipline it becomes the individual and the individual becomes it. This transition from Religion to Discipline is an advanced facet of the self and leads to higher states of self-knowingness. Once the pertinent union is objectified steady progress in religious practices and study are internalized and Religion no longer exists as separate or a part from the whole. Through the interacting of Discipline and Religious structure ritualistic practices fade into the suns of fundamentals. One becomes A Practicing Disciple of a discipline, which is Religion beyond Karma, and Effect, Astrology, Numerology, and all the rest. This union with religion and discipline is the junction where a person becomes Pure Cause. One enjoys a quiet ecstasy. There is no shouting, screaming, or catatonic flailing of arms. Becoming Pure Cause establishes union with the almighty."

In this stage of progression to higher self, lower self is annihilated completely and "I, My, and Mine" become the Impersonal self and the individual no longer exist." Claude interrupted, "Break time." She continued, "One becomes That."

He stepped outside the classroom and headed for the restroom. After relieving Himself He walked to the end of the hallway. There were several students engaged in conversation about a past class. He stood close enough to overhear what they were saying. The topic was wanting. A guy who He later found to be named Frahmad was laughing at some of the comments made by group members and they too were robustly laughing. He could not figure what the laughter was all about. How could they find a serious matter such as want a light matter? He stepped closer and listened with more intensity.

He was able to glean from the conversation the jocularity stemmed from a lecture given by Claude on instruction on the proper positioning of want and need.

It appeared the Imperialist had programmed the slaves to want. Wanting blinded the slaves to the reality of their diminished capacity. Wanting robbed the slaves of true reality. Through misapplied religious instruction slaves were taught to pray for whatever it was they wanted. This instruction is in definite contradiction to the Biblical teaching; "Thou shalt not want," means just that. "Do not want." Many of the slaves were lulled into believing God was supposed to give them what they wanted. Of course this was the wrong interpretation of the passage. So when their prayers were not realized they lost their faith in God.

This led them to believe in the slave master as being an okay guy. They were getting the best life had to offer, while being held hostage in a system that dehumanized them, and entrapped them in a vile vice of neo slavery. This precocious neo slavery included all ethnicities; it was colorblind. They did not know any better. A major part of the slave masters deception was convincing the slaves they were 'free. It was propagandized with regulated repetitions. The irony was saddening. Salvation came when people awoke and the truth of their condition was understood for what it was by the slaves.

Religion had transitioned in the same way as Education. It no longer focused on fear and reprisal. It was approached as the initial step one must leap into before tackling any thing else in life. The previous orientation with religion featured God as the worker and a vengeful monster. The new approach to it sought to inspire Men to be agents for God and fulfill his will by submitting their wills to his. Theologians, ministers, and all religious scholars agreed no pure success could be attained until one had found union with God. That was the starting point of your beginning. It was taught birth was the beginning of your exit to a new beginning. Therefore, your every act must ensure you are preparing for your exit. Success then became defined as finding Union with God before you exit life.

This preparatory addressing Religion highlighted living in the manner of the Word. The Religious rituals, ceremonies, and incantations of the old school religious wise were relegated to the significance of fundamentals when understood and exposed. Break ended and class resumed.

Upon returning to the classroom they briefly shared their comprehension of the lecture. Then, Claude gave them another assignment to prepare and bring to the next session. They left the classroom and stepped into that envelope of the Journey called life.

Chapter

4

PEACEKEEPERS

Frahmad called out to him as he was going out of the building, "Hey, you got a minute?" He paused and Frahmad came nearer extending his hand in a gesture of welcome. Frahmad told him everybody in the class had a study group. The group sizes were between five and eight people. The group Frahmad was in had only four people. They continued to talk as they walked to the tram stop; He agreed to join the study group. The group studied two evenings a week, for two hours. He could do that with ease. Plus, from what He saw He could use some catch up help. Although He had been exposed to some of what He heard in the class while incarcerated, this had more content. Frahmad caught the tram going North and, He crossed the street and waited for the East bound tram.

Later He found out Frahmad was a special individual indeed. During the Reconstruction all Countries, Nations, and Empires had to dismantle their Armies and Arms. It was agreed upon that a peace keeping force be assembled by the forming of a group of specially trained individuals from many Countries, Nations, and Empires. The only times these individuals would be together was for training.

Nine years prior-to the dissolution of the old system it was determined that eighty males and females would be formed to comprise a Peace keeping Force. They trained in the Himalayan Mountains with the Masters of the Mysteries of Life. After seven years of concentrated mind training each of them possessed the powers of teleportation, dematerialization, and highly refined telepathy. Garrotes were the weapons used to execute would be troublemakers. A visit from one of them was fatal. Their mission would always be to execute the leader of any organization whose intent was to Conquer, colonize, or enslave others.

It was rumored that Framad had recently returned from an assignment in Malaysia. All they knew for certain was the leader of an upstart movement of Communism had been successfully executed and Frahmad had missed one class.

A young man had begun speaking against Universalism and advocating a return to Communism. He claimed he had uncovered the ills that made Communism fail. He spoke with great diligence and apparently, many of the youths felt and believed the failures of Communism had no present time bearing. Youth in all ages has had its follies. The rebel's name was Hakidlu. He was in his mid thirties and very charismatic. As most upstarts he had little foundation for aspiring to return to a form of social living that had, time-and-time again, proven itself to be not only imprudent, but also inefficient in providing the necessary components for human development. Communism was good for providing basics, only. The Counselors and Committee knew, from research, observation and study, the higher purpose here was to grow and become One with the ONE.

In all ages and in all times there have been the young, the restless, the naive who have somehow deluded themselves into believing they have enough venerated wisdom and understanding to do a better job of auspice in the human experience. They all somehow miss the relevance of human development. History, as biased as it is, runs ramped with the trouble and mayhem these young pedants have brought about, and the aimless slaughter accompanying their efforts. For youth though it is blustery overflowing with vital vigor and freshest breath of life, will ever lay lacking in the consummate wisdom, experience and understanding of the mechanics of life.

Frahmad and his counter part had been after this young man for a day. He had gone into hiding; once it was made known he was to be eliminated. Frahmad and his partner carried a proclamation, which they presented to an official of Malaysia upon entering the province declaring the purpose of their mission its authorization, and its appropriateness. It would be laid upon the chest of Hakidlu once the execution was carried out. It would remain there for all, who had interest or concerns, to see for three days. It made it clear why the person was no longer among the people. It was official.

They found him cowering in a mineshaft. Hakidlu screamed, "Assassins! by what somber conscious do you come here to set me apart from my body?" Frahmad replied, "You have come to a place in your aspirations that demands you exit Body and life. In as much as you want to be somebody. Such aspirations usually end badly. Look at yourself! Your ambition has placed you in a mud hole awaiting execution. It is not 'i' who have set myself upon you, but you who have requested my presence and my task."

Hakidlu replied, "How difficult would it be for you to turn from this appointed proclamation and proclaim it done and finished?"

Frahmad responded, "Impossible! There is no place in me for a lie to find lodging. My existence finds truth as its only abode and necessity." In less than twenty-two hours the deed was done. Hakidlu's time on earth had come and gone. Frahmad and the others were well trained and instructed in submitting to the will of God.

The training they received rendered them impalpable, and incapable of error. They could pass through walls, appear and disappear at will, travel through time, space and ether in milliseconds, live without eating for months, one breath of air could sustain them for untold hours, by entering the body of any creature they could remove all negative spirits and energies in the universe and exit in less time than it takes to blink. Purified by the fires of understanding they were the epitome of spiritual ascension. Their very presence in any gathering, place, or situation was a healing and a mercy for all people and things. Above and beyond these attributes; they needed little and wanted less. Their will was the Will of the Creator. His thoughts returned to his own life and the present as the East Bound Tram halted. He entered.

Public transportation meant just that, it was free. Under reconstruction it was found feasible for transport from point to point be made free of charge. This was made possible by allocating funds from the GNP to a newly established Department of Conveyance and Transportation. He found a seat in the rear of the Tram and settled in for the ride home. Few people owned private transportation. Although limousines were available to all, He preferred to ride the Tram. Riding the Tram put Him in the company of people. He enjoyed watching them interact with each other. He could usually figure the stories of the lives of people on the Tram by observing their behavior and comments.

The tram zoomed along in a hum and He looked out the window. Before He went to the prison the area He was passing through had housing projects and crime ran rampant. Under the reconstruction all that had been done away with.

Reconstruction had relocated all the indigent and dispersed them as well. For the first time they were not all contained in the same areas of cities. Previously, they had been thrown together in living conditions unsuitable for raising 'pit bulldogs'. Public housing and housing authorities had finally admitted the lumping all the problems together was a bad idea. The redistribution of the troubled people made it impossible for gangs to nest. Add to that the punishment for being a gang member or congregating and consorting in gang manner discouraged gang affiliation too. No such thing as poverty existed and no gangs could be evidenced. Comfortable housing was a provision of the culture.

Some of adroit had assembled to evaluate the mortgage and lending institutions and determined they were more of a liability and hindrance than an asset and enhancement. Over time the reports, research, and finally the evaluation of these institutions proved beyond doubt, they were insolvent and had to be classified as Dinosaurs. An independent review board had to be assembled and convened to go over the conclusions before the decree was made final, that these institutions had to be dismantled. The effect of the change in housing was visible as everyone who got on the tram was bright and cheerful. The weight of being black mailed for shelter had produced a people of poor countenance and vile temperaments. Ill-tempered people are unable to maintain amenable social conditions. On the contrary, the old system fostered hostility and aggression among the people. The homicide rate kept growing and growing. At best it was vapid. Those conditions no longer existed.

When a person reached eighteen automatically lodgings were made available to them. Moderate lodgings were a guarantee for the rest of their lives. When the time came for the individual to start a family larger accommodations were available. There were contingencies in place to fit all human circumstances.

It was gratifying to see no homeless people begging on the street, and living in alleys. That was something worth dying for. It was accomplished without killing one person.

Chapter

5

MASS INSANITY

WHAT ENSUED FROM THE pedants establishing industrialization was mass insanity. It came at the costs of social development, harm to the environment, and most importantly self-realization. Industrialization infused competition among the people. They had to compete with one another for everything. Although it appeared they were free they were locked in mental cages and enclaves of beastly interactions. So they desperately engaged in activities that could anesthetize their brains. They drank alcohol, abused drugs, and had no sense of responsibility.

Upon reaching his apartment He met a female who lived in the same building. She invited Him to a party at one of her friend's parent's homes across town. The parents were away on vacation. Although, he had a lot to do, It was a chance to relax and enjoy something different.

It was a grand home, 3,000 square feet of living space. Although there were many people there it was orderly. Young and old mingled and socialized. One of the strengths of everybody having to continue to learn was a cross-index of age groups. In this party the unity of people was evident. Conversation flowed spontaneously and the mood was up beat yet peaceful. It was an open bar party and the food was arranged buffet style. The music was loud enough to be heard but not so loud people had to talk over it. The party went on through the night and into the early morning. He danced, ate, and drank Himself to sleep. Maybe it was the first party He had been to in many years. Maybe it was the thrill of it all. No matter what it was, He found it refreshing. He relaxed on a sofa in the insomnia room and fell asleep. When He awoke a full bosomed shapely flaxen haired beauty was kissing him softly on his neck and chest. She was invited Him to shower and refresh before heading home. He was spellbound by her beauty and willingly accepted her invitation.

They walked hand in hand into the master bedroom. She was removing her clothes step by step as they neared the master bathroom door. By the time they were inside the bathroom door she was completely naked. They showered and felt anew. He didn't exchange names with her. She had a way about her that qualified her to be in the high maintenance group. By no means was He about to enter that echelon of fast steppers. People in that set were forever chasing pleasure.

They were taught to pursue widgets and gigots, and sensual delights as symbols of triumph and success. The ruse was simple, efficient, and subtle. He was surprised that group was still around. They played handsomely into the hands of the Warlocks. The warlocks controlled who was eligible to get the most money[2] through many devious devices, in the old System. The people had to produce what the Warlocks manufactured as laborers or go lacking. In return the Warlocks paid them money to buy the things they produced, and to obtain their basics, as well. Upon receiving the money the people would, give it back to the warlocks. It was ingenious. The Warlocks were exchanging nothing for something.

The main problem with that System was, it was false and it caused a cycle of recession, depression and war. The Templars did

---

[2] Templars originally were King Richard III of England. In order to facilitate control of the wealth of the World for King Richard they created structured what was known as the currency or monetary system.

not see the metaphysical implications of the Monetary System. It was clever but false and consistently produced inconsistency. The Stipend Barter System produced consistency, among other Real Things.

The Stipend System allotted every person an equal portion of the wealth of the World, at age eighteen. This was done, by depositing equal shares of the World Wealth in a Central Crediting Account monthly. It stabilized daily living. However, under no circumstances could anyone or any group accrue extremely large amounts of credits. The Stipend System was not intended to give anything other than balance to living. It was a Number System structured on Parity.

Instinct told many something was drastically wrong with the Monetary System; but they could not put their finger on it. So they got drunk, abused drugs, killed one another, raped women and children, engaged in same sex relations, created trash, disturbed the ecological balance, engaged in recreational sex, and manifested all the symptoms of insane and disingenuous roles of being. The elite and top levels sought girls as young as five for sex in other parts of the world. They high signed on one another and drove many to inject addictive substances in their arms, legs, genital areas, and made the illegal lawful and acceptable. In one Organized Religion priest preyed upon young boys for sex with such zeal one would incline it held a special positive power. It didn't. It discredited the Religion.

The education they received prepared them to labor for money, in the warlocks' pyramid of slavery. It was far from education. Instead of educating them, it drove them further into insanity. Some such as He knew it for what it was from childhood and fought it, every step of the way. He refused to play by their rules. It made no sense to Him that He should live in squalor by dent of another's explanation. How could He abide by a set of rules that made it okay for possessions to be legally taken and it be illegal for the possessions to taken back. It was Witch Craft and He knew it.

His encounters with formal Education shed darkness on darkness, for Him. He was introduced to phonetics in the first grade. It was a very uncomfortable acquaintanceship. The teacher told him, "The numeral 1 was spelled O-N-E." This contradicted the phonetic rules she had taught Him earlier. As His formal education continued He found words had letters in them that were silent. To his embarrassment as a human, others were okay with this dissociative programming they were being forced to swallow. He could see it. Why couldn't they see it? They were, by any means, being miss educated. They were being programmed or conditioned to conform rationally to contradictory sounds, symbols, and stimuli that defied reason and logic. They were being put to sleep. Their self-reliance was being ripped from their bosoms with clandestine guile. Slowly over time they were required to forsake portions of themselves and sink into dark and murky abysses of self-denial and abandonment to obtain that which they were entitled to have privy to as a birth rite. Their natural instinct was being compromised. He found the programming unacceptable. It all came to a head when He was in his teens.

His dilemma with the, so-called, Justice System could've began when He was seventeen. His father had worked for a company for twenty-five years and suddenly the company went out of business. It happened at a time when the country was in a recession and jobs were scarce. He had eleven brothers and sisters. His father had fourteen mouths to feed. His father's unemployment ran out and things got ugly. Eventually, the bank foreclosed on their home, and they were tossed in the street.

His father took it hard. He had paid diligently for the home every month for eighteen years and through no fault of his it was being taken away from him. He only had four more years to make the payments and the home would have been free of any debt; it would've been his. Instead he was being evicted, made homeless. It was legal for the bank to take the home from His father. It was illegal for His father to take the home back from the bank. This typical duality was a primary trait of the old system. It lulled the people into thinking, even believing they had control of their lives and the things they were using, only to rip them away at a moments notice.

The people never realized the things they sought to own or possess were manipulating them. The truth of it was revealed when they came to the realization of their being controlled by the things they had, temporary custody of. The wake up call for his father was too much. The thin thread most people dangle by proved inadequate to sustain him. It snapped. With it's snapping his father went into a downward spiral. A bottomless pit opened and he plummeted down, down into an overwhelming darkness that wrenched all hope from his heart. His father destitute and despondent saw no way out; up, or back took his life by asphyxiation. It was all he could afford. Between donations and whatever they could scrape together they raised enough money for a paupers funeral for their Patriarch. There wasn't enough money to put a head stone on the grave. The only identifying mark at the gravesite was the six-inch concrete circle location marker used by the graveyard, lot 8 site 56.

Accepting the living structures and conditions under which they lived was insane. He could not come to terms with the circumstances that drove His father to start the car and close the garage door. His father had played by the rules. The system failed His father and His family. In twenty-five years of helping another create and maintain a Life Style, His father had not missed one day. Nobody gave a damn. He was expendable to help His Father as were all the rest of the sleeping giants. The only sane thing left to do was take the Bull by the horn. He chose to step further outside the rules.

After the burial He stood at the gravesite, growing angrier as the shinny cars drove out of the cemetery and life continued on for some. In His mines eye was the spot under the bridge where His family had temporary shelter now. There was only one thing to do.

It didn't take long for Him to get to the spot under the bridge. No sane person would accept dehumanization as overt as this. In a moment of lucidity He saw His choice as the most logical, rational, and sane choice on the table. He rummaged through the boxes of their goods and found a long sharp kitchen knife. He shoved the knife in His pants and hurriedly left the area before any family member questioned Him.

He jogged and walked fast. His heart was pounding in His chest; partially from anger and partially with. His body trembled and His footing was unsteady. His vision was blinded with rage and His intent was pure raw vengeance. He arrived at the bank that had foreclosed on their home. The bank was fairly empty. There was a middle age man standing at a teller window. The security guard was drinking a cup of coffee, and the bankers were busy at their desks.

He walked up behind the middle age man and put the knife to his throat. He told the teller, "This is a stick up! Give me all you got or the man dies!" He told the security guard to take off his gun belt and place it on the floor. Then, kick it over to Him. He made everybody lie face down on the floor, except the teller. He picked up the gun and gun belt. He hid the gun and belt under his tee shirt. He told the teller to fill up a moneybag with what was in her till. He tucked the moneybag in the back of His pants and existed the bank. An elderly gentleman was about to enter the bank, as He existed. He stopped him and asked Him in a frenzied voice, "Did you see him, huh did you see him? I think he went up town! He just robbed the bank!", Bewildered the man entered the bank saying, "What's going on?" "I think the robber went up town," He said. There was much confusion in the Bank. Everybody in the Bank was either in shock or a nervous wreck. Someone had presences to push the alarm button and within minutes the police were there.

He took off in the direction of downtown and two blocks later turned south. Using back streets and short cuts He would be hard to trace. He had layered His clothes so He looked much larger than He was. As He moved about, in His get away, He discarded a jacket and hood. When He reached the downtown section of town He stopped in a restaurant and ate lunch. Sirens were screaming through the town and heads were turning in anticipation of pending excitement. Hour and a half later things quieted down, considerably. He left the restaurant and took in a movie. It was a double feature, so when He came out of the theatre it was dark. Under the cover of darkness He proceeded to complete His get away. His get away was clean. After about an hour He felt His old self again.

The take was $10.000.00 plus. It wasn't enough to take care of the family for long, but it was a start. Within a month the family was no longer on the street. He told his Mother a lie and she was in no condition, mentally, to question Him. In His mind right and wrong were no longer clearly definable by any standard other than what He had set. He understood right depended upon who had the upper hand and made the rules. The legal system abided by the rules scribed in the rule book and turned a jaundiced eye upon true right and wrong. It was the good old boys club out of control, as usual. He did not make the rules, but He was going to do His best to find success in the game. In all truth the justice system was not concerned with people committing crimes. It just wanted crime to continue. The wrong was getting caught, not the act itself. The system was crooked. It was not designed to prevent crime.

He got together with two young men who found themselves in the same boat. They planned a robbery that could not be reported to the cops. During the robbery there were a few anxious moments, times when time stood still. The three of them netted four and a half million dollars. They split the money three ways.

With part of His share He bought a vacant building in His neighborhood. He was too young to buy it in His name so it was bought in His mother's name. He made a modest down payment. The building was located near some hot nightspots. It was four stories high with a parking lot in the rear that the nightclubs used as an overflow parking lot. He converted the second, third, and part of the forth floors for parking to. It had a freight elevator in the rear and a loading dock. He refurbished the elevator so it suited the clientele of the Night Clubs. Each floor had an area of 4,250 square feet of space.

There was no car detailing shop in the area, so He opened a complete one on the first floor. At age twenty He was doing fine, financially. As family members came of age He brought them into the business as staff and His business became the talk of the town. Customer satisfaction was the product He vended. People far and near came to Him to get their cars detailed.

Things were going so well He still had most of the money from the big heist. The businesses afforded Him cash flow, which enabled Him to up grade the standard of His family's life style. Without exposing Himself to investigation by government agencies. Then, came a problem.

Ronnie, one of the three became a victim of the Casino's lure, fast life, bright lights, swift women, and blew through his money in two years. Casinos were giving him the blues and he began to lean on Him and the other guy. Ronnie owed the Casinos big time. The pressure was great and Ronnie did not want to be killed. It was either pay up or vanish permanently. He was scared. Now Ronnie was threatening to tell the drug dealers who robbed them. The three of them met and discussed their options. The best option was another escapade. Somehow the idea didn't bother Him. In America crime was encouraged. It was the getting caught that was discouraged. Even getting caught only amounted to a slap on the wrist, if you had enough money.

A day later He was on his way to the engine steam cleaning area when one of His customers stopped Him. They got into a discussion about the big accident that happened the day before. It was alleged a drunk driver had crossed the freeway and ran head in into a school bus, which overturned and spun out into three cars, which were collided into by eleven cars and a big rig. In all nine children were killed, thirty-four people were hospitalized in critical condition and a total of sixteen people were treated at the scene. The bus driver was pronounced dead at the scene and seven adults who were in their cars and the big rig were seriously injured. The drunk did not have a scratch. They both agreed alcohol had played a big part in this accident and was a terrible drug. It so happened the person who stopped Him worked for the bureau of Alcohol Firearms and Tobacco. During the conversation it came out that there was a large shipment of alcohol being delivered to the central warehouse in two weeks. The street value of the load was in the neighbor hood of $ 700,000.00 dollars. The guy was very forth coming with all the particulars including, date, and time of arrival, size, and description of the common carrier. It was a night delivery and the driver had a habit of stopping for dinner at truckers stop, 55 miles outside of the city. There was plenty open space between the city and the truck stop.

With this information He met with the other two and planned a high jacking. Before they decided to pull-off the highjack they had to find buyers. Getting rid of the booze was as critical as ripping it off. The search began for liquor stores, bars, hotels, restaurants, casinos, holes in the walls, bootleggers, and after hour joints interested in buying hot booze. The word got out fast by way of "the grape vine." Before long they had sold 1,500 cases of the load. It was such an appealing deal that many buyers paid for their orders in advance. In the community He was known for honesty and trustworthiness. The remaining cases they could use themselves. It would be their share of the high jacking. The money from the high jacking would go to get Ronnie strait with Vegas. They needed to get Ronnie off the hook with Vegas and off their backs.

Timing and planning had to be impeccably coordinated. There was no room for mistakes and it had to work. This would be the last hurrah! Ronnie would have to get himself together and grow up. The immature cavorting had to stop. It was explained in cold hard language to Ronnie, he had to make the best of this haul or The Casinos would not be his only problem.

The trick required seven paneled trucks, a ramp ten feet long, a pallet jack and seven drivers. The spot was 35 miles from the city. It was a road that rigs traveled to get to a small town. A rig on that road would not be noticed or reported to the highway patrol. Midway between the small town and the highway was a stand of trees. The rig could be hidden there while it was unloaded into the panel trucks. Seven trucks would be standing by to haul the booze from the spot to the buyers. The transfer could be made in less than seventy-five minutes. They practiced every step of the plan and after a week they got the time down to forty-five minutes.

It was one of the inanest moments of his life. He was acting like the masses, insane. Things appeared to be back to normal for three years, after the heist. Then, one day Ronnie stormed into His office in frenzy. Ronnie had blown his money again. They argued. The argument escalated into a fistfight. In the brawl He hit Ronnie and knocked him down. Before Ronnie landed on the floor his head struck the corner of an end table. The corner of the table punctured his temple and he was pronounced dead at the scene. He was tried for involuntary manslaughter, and found guilty as charged. Subsequently He was sentenced to three to five years in state penitentiary. He got into a couple of fights and wound up doing the entire five-year stretch. He was twenty-three when He went to prison.

Chapter

6

RECONSTRUCTION

DURING THE RECONSTRUCTION PERIOD International Human Development Council was convened to construct a system devoted to the development of human sociability. In order to eliminate War from Mans' learned or programmed behavior of the past times, all people had the same goal; end war and find Liberation. Which is realizing the attainment of the state of absolute "Being." Absolute Being is waking with your hand in God's hand through life.

Somebody finally woke up and realized the problems confronting humans stemmed from fundamentally defective adults in the maturation stage of being. Mature adults enjoy peace and know it to be a very closeness to God. The liberated have matured to the consciousness of unconditional existence, simply "Being."

Little Children have great difficulty sharing things. Immature adults have the same problem. Many adults never reach maturity in human development or lose me, me, self-absorption upon attaining adulthood.

The inability to devise a method of sharing equally the Wealth of the earth stems from flaws in under developed character, or immaturity. Self-absorption is a learned behavior. It is one manifestation of Self-Absorption. Since it is a learned behavior it is correctable. It can be disentangled from character and when this occurs Character begins to develop. The advantage for the development of humans is humans mature quicker and enjoy more unity. Any behavior that is learned can be unlearned. It takes time and proper guidance to change unacceptable behavior.

It was apparent the goal of life had to be redefined in support of the necessary changes. The standard for evaluation of humans achieving maturity in social development had to clearer and less abstract. More than that it had to be measurable. Some of the most advanced African Cultures had set a measurable standard. **"Measuring how well humans were getting along together and how well humans were taking care of one another;"** that would be the definer of human evolutionary advancement, technology had been the definer of Mans' advancement. Technology has now been defined as a distraction, and a major distraction. It had found its rightful place, a gadget and widget supplier. It never was an indicator of advancement. On the contrary, it merely attested to Man gullibility.

A selection committee had to be organized to determine who would make up the Council. The committee members were not eligible for positions on the Council of Elders themselves. It would convene at the site of the Parthenon, Temple of Athena, in Greece. Men and women who had attained Understanding of Human Being and a fervent familiarity with the Ultimate Success Life Afforded gathered. The wise, the formally educated scholars, and pedants were welcome, too.

In all forty-two people, out of five hundred fifty-seven, made the cut. Of that group twelve would make up the Council of Elders and seven would be designated alternates. It would be a lengthy process. The same committee selected the individuals who made up the Council of Elders. There would be seven alternates who would attend all sessions, but in total silence. After the groupings were established an independent agent presented them with their Goal. It was Using, 'Do unto others as one would have others do unto them' as a framework for interdependent living to achieve improvement in human development. It would entail close scrutiny over how well we were getting along together and how well we were treating each other. It was the framework for the project. What's more it was visually measurable and overtly assessable.

The invitees were people who challenged the principles of Colonization, the validity of Exploration, and the Social Stratification constructs. They had studied Man and his journey from every aspect of development. They were humble people, people who were principled in human decency as well as preservation of their species. They were well acquainted with Truth, and as humble as the dirt on the ground. No college degree was necessary as a qualification for candidacy. Having insight into universal self was a critical qualification. They were those who walk among us unnoticed. Endued by the Creator with illumination they lived to serve as his agents, only. All else in life holds no purpose, for them.

Over a seventy-five year period these Divinely inspired ones lit the Path as never before. Alternates had to be searched for and brought into the fold. The Council of Elders raised the acceptable behavior standards for human behaviors. In keeping with human's higher nature, they responded favorable and rose to meet the expectations. Ideas of ownership were replaced with the reality of usage. Material things were regarded as responsibilities and deserving of care. They were no longer possessions as objects owned. Simplicity became the new Path to the Riches of the Life Experience. First, An examination of Anthropology might reveal much of the relative science to being Man was devoted to spiritual development by the Ancients. Second, simplicity was identified as a key component in self-discovery.

This led to separating the Real from the mere Functional, i.e. a watermelon, is Real, an invented thing, is a Forms of Function. The Council of Elders introduced the Stipend System to replace the Monetary and Banking Systems. Not only was it a better method of maintaining Peace and Harmony, it eliminated Poverty and Secured unity. It also, made man safer from his own species. Making Man safer from his own species was not a characteristic of money. The use of money was primarily functional as a means of controlling the many by the few. Money and invented things were the manipulating strings of the Puppeteers. They took far more out of life than they put into life. They had the appearances of giving and all the time they were taking. The Real in life is ever balancing and contributing to the experience of living.

The unreal things in life are ever unbalancing and destroying. They coincide with the insane antics of the non-believers and the misguided. The Real is ever balancing and monitoring.

Those two had to be identified and separated before the contrition for past repetitious acts would be erased. The lessons held in the breast of the past had to finally yield their harvest. Standing on their merit and being judged for results their lessons keys and guides for Man's mission, they pointed the way. It was the advent of form of function that made man become beguiled and lose his way. Not one step forward could be possible until this impostor was revealed.

Using divers methodologies magicians, warlocks,

Demons, Maya, and Satan had interposed forms of function for Reality. It was diabolical. Further, it would require close scrutiny to keep form of function out of the realm of possibility for the morrow.

It was concluded and adopted as well founded practice to disavow anything as real that did not have the ability to reproduce itself, naturally. This distinction placed items and objects manufactured or artificially produced into the category of forms of function. Meaning they were tangible and served some limited purpose which, was neither totally necessary, nor partially necessary for human lives and life as well to continue. Included in the category of forms of function were manufactured or mass-produced products that had proven to be incompatible with the environment. The production of such items had to be limited. This led to a reassessment of the goal of education and accelerated the educational thrust to the ends of self-mastery. The old system had as its aim, producing people who were selfish. They were programmed to be ignorant of themselves.

Previously, the most intelligent people used an average of seven percent of their brains. The first thing that had to be done was destroying all the books on education. A curriculum was developed that would not only awaken the unused portion of the brain, but also nourish it. Subsequently, the human development out stripped the need for many items serving as forms of function. This change reduced the amount of trash and waste which technology had made as normal and tolerable. Man became aware of his true existence as unlimited in being and doing. The transition was not well received by the slave masters.

Change has always met with resistance. The slave masters hated to give man his due accord. Miss education made it an easy task for the Slave Masters to keep man in a state of reliance and dependence on them. Miss education had man focusing on Acquisition of controlling and possessing temporal things. This miss education denied Man access to an awareness of his true being. The blocking of this awareness made it impossible to be self. In reality Man's efforts was best directed at finding his way home, which is not of the Physical World. Man's ultimate entitlement was determined to be the opportunity to find his way home, to his source. The use of money coupled with intentional miss education impeded that. Instead of having time for his development in that area he had to busy himself chasing money and conducting himself in servitude to the slave masters. Those in control of money made sure Man would never have enough to get the opportunity to rid himself of his oppressors. The relationship between the money controllers and the controlled was simple parasitism. Over time the parasites proved to be unsuccessful, because they destroyed their hosts.

In the back recesses of his mind Man knew there had to be a better way. Without money he was unable to have food, clothing, shelter, safety, true love, or self-esteem. Money was highly liquid and some would rob and kill for it. It created more problems than it satisfied. It did not serve as means of exchange, for goods and or labors, at all. On the contrary it was a device whereby the parasites could control the daily functions and lives of Man. Its role in the mix was to help the greedy and made poverty possible. Money had to go. The only acceptable means of exchange among humans was declared to be Barter.

Change is always active. A system had to be put in place that would minimize the stature of money in the journey. A Stipend system was adopted. It worked. It had been implemented fifteen years after the securing Universal Health Care. As a result of its effect, the levels of human harmony were rising markedly every single year. It was certain this change was indicative of improved problem solving by Man. They were making strides in caring for one another. Each Man could see himself in his fellowman. Each Man cared for each man as his brother, and Peace abided.

The term Mankind would no longer reference all of humanity. It would identify a type of man; specifically adamant to Man and opposed to his welfare. It would represent exactly what the word contains in its seven letters, "A kind of man." The character and characteristics of mankind were defined as, 'One who impersonates man and is purposefully conspiring to deter man from his Goal of attaining oneness with his Creator.' Man was redefined as Spiritual Beings cast in the image of God searching for unification with his Creator.

These changes without a doubt were met with great and strenuous truculence. No matter the opposition, the changes had to take place. The world was being rocked, ravaged, and ripped apart by the manipulative sway of money and miss education. Mankind had given money a power that was nonexistent, after all it was no more real, and of no more of value than a piece of paper with ink on it. At one time money was backed by precious metals. An elaborate justification was devised to explain the value of the metals. Only, a miss educated person may find validity in such a hoax. Life could and would continue without it. It was not a necessity. It only served as an Office of advantage to the stingy, lazy, the socially deficient and the sociological degenerate people.

Ownership was also a problem of some great concern, too. Another blunder of miss educating people was the redundant and repeated impregnation of the idea of ownership. Possession does not constitute anything beyond having use of something. When this reality was educated properly, improved human harmony was be the result in a short span of time. Theoretically, it was possible to own temporal things. This was a harmful theory. It nurtured "Iness and Myness." Some men's overzealous drive to own what others were using were acknowledged as primary motivators for War. In truth this **idea** did more to obstruct reality than it did to clarify it. Having animate and inanimate things in your possession and under your control does not constitute ownership. The idea is bogus. It constitutes the privilege to use something for a period of time, with some degree of exclusion. More importantly, using things constitutes a great degree of responsibility. In reality the possibility of literal ownership was fallacious. It was determined one could use things, only. Things were subject to their command and control in use, only. This proper education became the foundling child of increased maturity, responsibility, and accountability.

Welcoming the position of use of things vaulted innocence into its proper position on man's journey to Ultimate Success, Union with God. Money and ownership drove innocence from man's conscious aspirations. It was replaced with greed, guile, treachery, deception, deceit, and the most grievous disfigurements of 'the Real,' desiring and wanting.

Innocence accords man a thrust into being that seeks harmony with all that is. The more in harmony Man is with all of creation the more of himself he is. Innocence is that dynamic, which unlocks the door concealing the transition from finite the world of limitations to the infinite world outside of limits. Innocence girds the indignities in fine silk tapestry and melds them into slop suitable for mud hole swine. Through the purifying fires of innocence the trust barriers are removed and fear is abated. It ascends to the one becoming the many, and the many becoming the ONE. Subsequently, war, violence, hidden agendas, threats, bullying, extortion, blackmail, and man's lower nature are unable to exercise command over acts, and incidents. In short, by its nature, innocence promotes human advancement that is measurable.

Technology as well as progress demonstrates man kind's stupidity. As of this date they have contributed to ecological imbalance, trash, and pollution stand as proof of man kind's special brand of stupidity. The residual remains of special stupidity are waste, trash, and pollution. Worldwide man kind, resorted to producing tons and tons of trash as he strove to get rich. The gigots Man Kind produced in those days were obsolete within three months of introduction into the market place. Innocence gone from his soul he produced inferior goods to realize humungous, rapid, and sequential financial gains. He no longer concerned himself with any other priority than greed, greed, and more greed. The rebirth of innocence evolved out of necessity. Otherwise the doom's day bell would have been sounding far and near. The new system would have to divest itself of many old and inadequate practices and institutions. It posed a Herculean task, never the less, it had to be done. At no other time in the history of man had a few assembled to right a sinking ship of this enormity.

The greatest assault on innocence was evidenced by the fact that money afforded three repugnant things, greed, control of others, and unrivaled in enormity the pangs of wanting. Wanting spawn trash, sin, and deceit. En masse people were storing stuff in storage lockers. Money had made it impossible to resist buying the newest gadget and storing the old one. Most of the storage lockers were so jam packed with stuff a person could only open the door and toss in the latest treasure. In all too many cases, the people had no idea what they had stored in the rear of the lockers. One thing was fairly certain, the treasures stored in the rear of the storage bens, had very little chance of seeing daylight for quite some time. Greed and the tendency to hoard were the driving force, as the sole reward, for the despair that accompanies wanting led them to. They were unable to see wants are unlimited. Wanting had gotten the upper hand and need lay trammeled in the dust of confusions of distraction and deception.

It was plain the majority of stuff in the storage locker would eventually be in a landfill. The ruse was out of control. Many had found justification for hoarding by claiming these discards would be antiques someday. Expecting to gain profit from trash and discards is just another form of greed. The study revealed, antiques are slow sellers and have never flown off retailers' shelves in great quantities. The greatest clue to the stuff in the storage locker being just so much trash is this, to be an antique the item must have been hand made by an artisan of some distinction. Ninety-nine percent of the stuff in the storage lockers was mass-produced in factories. The rest, the one percent, was made by, "Who gave a care?" It had no potential to be anything but trash. People were being manipulated and exploited in great numbers by the parasites and did not even know it. Through miss education the parasites had purposefully led the slaves into a state of ignorance concerning entitlements. It would be some time before a significant portion of the slaves could shed the shackles of denial the parasites had ensnarled them in. The greatest deceiver of the miss education process is, it presents wanting as an equal to needing.

The Bible teaches wanting is doing business with the Devil. Why is this the case with wanting? Wants are unlimited and incapable of ever giving peace, contentment or saturation. A Want is a device. It is an insufferable device that is incapable of ever reaching satiety. The more one seeks to appease it or host it the more outrageous it becomes. It is a trap. Scripture cautions against waste and want in two sentences "Waste not." "Want not." These two sentences are simple enough to be self-explanatory. The difficulty in devising proper interpretation of the words comes from the in ability of those entrusted with teaching the meanings. The first two words advise man, not to waste. The second two words advise man not to want. Yet, Man blindly ignored those words repeatedly and created trash at an unbelievable rate. Trash was the net result of man's pursuit of the things that lured him. Things to want had the day. Trash was smothering the earth. Money made this travesty possible. The practice of fulfilling the wants of man by tendering money was proven not only woeful to man, but also it was devastating to the very earth he was dependent on for his existence and sustenance as well. Profiteering took precedence over preservation of the earth. Without a doubt, money had to go.

An example of improper interpretation of words may be seen in the following example: *"In Kenya there were certain areas that were vital to the communities. These areas were designated as 'no man's land' because they were commonly shared. When the Europeans arrived their interpretation of no man's land meant it was up for grabs by the first opportunist."* Naturally, the two indifferent interpretations of the same words created a problem, which was quickly resolved by the Europeans resorting to violence. Get the point?

Need had to come to the for upon man's beginning to recapture innocence. So it began. Want was identified as an enemy to man. It was relegated to a position of insignificance in human development, and no longer catered to.

Chapter

7

THE GIFT

THE COUNCIL HELD THAT man was given a gift at birth from his Creator. Development of his gift will always prove adequate to sustain man. His gift is his ability to make positive contribution to the social development of his species. His constructive contributions earn man the right to be alive. In social collectives that are conducive to human development it works well. His gift improves the world around him and everyone benefits. When shared with his fellows who understand developing self, it is not only euphoric in nature, but also vital to the arrival of the transcendent states of consciousness men are heir to.

During His imprisonment, He tried His hand at different things. He knew He had to reform and develop or His time in life would be shortened. He understood He had failed to develop earlier in life. He had confused age with maturity. The content of life is awakened in man's maturing. He had wasted the earlier part of His life chasing shadows, i.e. fame and fortune. There was no place for those two charlatans in the new system. In the new system there was no sympathy for unacceptable behaviors, or clemency. Each man was defined by his acts. Therefore each man had to earn the right to be alive. Man had to grow up and enjoy the feast by behaving himself, or suffer famine by behaving inappropriately. That was it. What a person did spoke for itself. The excuse clinics were no longer regarded as glamorous or practical. The Deed spoke for itself.

The idiomatic expression, "earning a living," was defrocked. It cannot be done. No one can earn a living. The idea was gross insanity. It implied, earning oodles of money might extend life. It is possible to create a life style, or earn the right to be alive. Earning a living just cannot be done. Those who chose to be a problem for the people working to earn the right to be alive were to be executed summarily. There was a dramatic shift in focus. Humans were focusing on earning the right to be alive.

He tried carpentry and cut himself, hit His hand with hammers, nearly lost some fingers using a skill saw, and wasted, a large amount of lumber. Not one skill in the, entire construction field had any fascination for Him. He tried cooking school and discovered the only thing to enjoy was either tasting or eating. After many ventures He went back to carpet weaving.

It felt right. There were no conditions or standards to be met; it had a liberating appeal about it. It was creative and it made Him feel close to His Maker. He lost himself every time He began to create a carpet. He was there and not there at the same time. Soon, He was merely an observer of the creation He was working on. Each carpet He finished was more beautiful than the previous one. No matter how dark the colors were the carpet held a hypnotic glow all over. He had found His gift. Owing to the new system He could readily afford to trade these carpets for things the system did not provide, without difficulty.

The word got out about his gift and people waited patiently for one of his carpets. Some provided services for him such as hair cuts for a year. Others Exchanged promised massages for a period of time. The trading for his carpets and rugs was a joy for all. The glow of his works was not unusual. Typically all the work done in the society by people who had arrived at their gift from the Creator had similar characteristics. It was the energy of the person who had realized union with the ONE. For the first time in the life experience groups of humans saw glowing in their works as the standard level of production. The new system appreciated the people who made or crafted things. They were living examples of being at a level whereby they and the work were one. Inanimate objects took on aspects of blissful life in their hands.

There was so much of Him in His works that it was reported, Standing on one of His carpets and looking just three feet ahead of your feet, it was possible to exit your body and go anywhere in the entire Universe. The transitions out of body made available access to the traveler the language of the people as well as their traditions, festive occasions, and folkways. Some reported after an out of body experience, from one of His rugs, upon return they had no need to eat for two weeks. Others claimed they could smell the fragrances of not only the incense, from the meditation centers they visited, but also the scent of the punks the incense was attached to. Many proclaimed the attainment of a cleansing of spirit previously unrealized in any measure.

The learned claimed these things were possible because ingenuously His weave and rhythmic pattern had found harmony with universal light. As is common in such unions the connection secures closure between all that is with all that is. Then it is possible to be everywhere and nowhere at the same time. It is in this state of consciousness that Non-Being is realized.

This transformation or fusion of spirit into the carpets gave universal light to the darkness of yesterday's, spiritual mysteries. Life showered the reality of light and spirit shinning softly onto the world. There was laughter everywhere and life was blissful. The world was transformed into a stage for acting out the life to come, peace, trust, and truth designed the scripts of the role players. People began to awaken to the light of their power to cause peace on earth. The discovery gave every person's being as equally important.

Chapter

8

MARRIAGE

PROFESSOR CLAUDE ANDERSON PLUNGED into a lecture on marriage and its role in the human experience. Primarily, "The family is the most important institution in any society. It should be preserved at all costs. The roles in a marriage need to be defined and strictly adhered to. Until now there had been no, culture of record, that was healthy accept among indigenous people. Historically, history reveals what happens to a people when the culture is disregarded. It becomes unhealthy and dies. Members of a culture need to accept the roles as practiced by the culture. Failures to respects male and female roles to the commission of acts not scripted will result in dissolution of the marriage, and over time the culture. Destruction of the family precedes the destruction of a culture.

Cultures are very fragile things. The substance of a culture is, "It's a story being lived by a group of people." To maintain healthy cultures roles must be clearly defined and adhered to. As fragile as it is cultures determine the type of government needed to impose upon the people. In cultures that are advanced government has very limited hands on duty. Government has a mighty hand in underdeveloped or behind in human development cultures. Deviation from culturally scripted norms, mores, folkways, and customs are signs of cultures with a terminal illness. Culturally, developed roles encourage the discovery of Reality. When a person looks into either a mirror of calm body of water the image there is the being that resides in the body. Scripted roles make it much easier to be that.

Characteristics of underdeveloped cultures are cultures where there is a great deal of role stain for members, role conflict for members and exploitation, and lastly miss education, instead of human development. The demeanor of underdeveloped cultures is deviant norms that suggest social insanity, i.e. war incest, lying, cheating, and dishonesty.

Therefore the structure of marriage must be thoroughly thought out and as simple to conform to as humanly possible." By the role being carefully thought about, there is nothing to think about, as far as changing it. The benefit here is, not having to think about the role takes a lot off the mind.

Upon conclusion of the class, we were given team assignments. Each team would meet and share the benefits of Monogamy and Polygamy. The criteria for assessing benefit would be how well the one or the other served the benefit of humans evolving into a oneness with their Creator.

There was another part to this assignment. The teams had to prepare an in depth assessment that would validate the benefits Monogamy potentially had over Polygamy, as far as neutralizing role strain, role conflict, exploitation, and miss education. In a future session polygamy would be presented, and its potential to neutralize cultural ills would be given equal time. A final session on the subject would be necessary to determine which of the two could be associated as real and which was form of function. By this time the students had enough life experience to know form of function always was a source of short term or long term damages, and should be minimally applied.

What He found amazing was the no test structure, and no grade structure, of the new form of education. A person was expected to provide evidence of some level of improved proficiency in the study area by preparing a presentation. Surprisingly enough there were many methods that ably proved proficiency verification. Formal Education was focused on spiritual development. It replaced forced education and was for the individual development of self-control.

All five team members were excited about the assignment and began the project eagerly. Although the new system embraced polygamy, they understood why monogamy warranted examination. They met at His apartment.

The first issue in marriage is the purpose of marriage?. Frahmad responded, "Marriage is the union formed by males and females for the wholesome reproduction, modeling and extension of the human species. The cement that holds the marriage together is friendship. Love comes over time provided the two people can trust each other. In turn, trust is born and cared for then love has a holiday. In this time and in this place we have rejected monogamous marriages for its inability to prevent certain human frailties, i.e. lying, rape, statutory rape, child molestation, homosexuality, adultery, unwanted children, and prostitution. It weakens marriage and makes the unhealthy choices of frivolity more attractive than ever." Humans need to be allowed to have sex with partners other than their spouses, males and females.

Sheila interrupted saying, "She did not see how polygamous unions could prevent those negatives from occurring."

Her statement was made before she had all the facts clearly explained to her. Once she had the proper understanding of it, she agreed it was the better choice.

He asked her, "Can you state your position or understanding in common language that validates polygamous unions as wholesome and necessary." She laughed and replied, "We will certainly find out when my turn comes to present, won't we?"

At that point Rhonda chimed in with, "Claude laid heavy emphasis on the importance of role play in marriage. Claude was very careful in the presentation of how important it was to assist ones mate in being successful in their roles." The importance of this support can never be overstated though it is heralded day in and day out throughout all eternities. Role-play in daily living prevents unwholesome reproduction and negative perpetuation of the human species. It removes the frailty of emotions and substantiates proper actions. Anthropological studies of parts of African Communities, prior to 1600, contained many ceremonies that were traditions and served more of a purpose than a salute to words. These traditions were passed from generation to generation as the Way of the elders. It was held these traditions would light the way of dark passage for the young to find the elders in the next life. At the same time they had the capability to produce healthy male female relationships in this life, and perpetuate strong cultures to further evolve I the next.

The failure of these cultures to flourish and continue in a healthy fashion came about by a disease. The indigenous people were proclaimed savages, because of their innocence by the invaders and intruders who stumbled upon them.

Marriage constitutes a change in behavior. People that marry and continues to behave as though they were single are experiencing role conflict. Unless they are able to realize their dilemma, the marriage is domed.

In the old system this little item was completely overlooked. Even though most young men had a bachelor party, they did not understand the significance of the event. It announced the end of being single. It ushered in the beginning of husband hood. The roles are completely different. Spouses spend time bonding with their spouses and becoming one unit, family. Marriage requires maturity and self-control. Bachelors spend time with the guys talking about women and playing games together, and enjoying immaturity. It was difficult to get beyond the old programming of being out of control, or doing whatever you want to do as the real deal. The failure of many monogamous marriages was directly attributed to the individuals' inability to modify their behavior to fit the role of marriage.

There was no clarity in role differentiation, subsequently the divorce rates were extremely high and nobody understood why.

Males were marrying and continuing to live as if they were single. At worst males treated the relationship with spouses as living with their mothers.

Under the new system marriage education was an intricate part of the social development curriculum class. It was reinforced in the life styles of the wedded people in the community. One of the amazing discoveries of all ages was, self-discipline was not the enemy to true being. Of course none of it works without truth. This change in education greatly reduced the divorce rate.

That is why the accepted marriage was restricted to polygamy. At no time in the chronicles of man have there been more men on the planet than women. Every woman needs to have the fulfilling joy of motherhood. To prevent men from skulking around having sexual relations with unwed females, it was permitted for men to have more than one spouse. There were conditions and provisions that had to be met. As far as it being one sided, it was not the case. The females could have sexual relations with other men as long as it was done openly. The wisdom in this adaptive arrangement eliminated two taboos, prostitution and adultery. It gave dignity to sexual relations.

Francine broke in saying, "It is amazing how much pure liberation is built into polygamy. I mean, a way of life that gives approval of lust clearly allows love to stand apart from sex, in the carnal sense, while providing bridled control over our lower desires. I like it, I am glad we don't live under that monogamous structure. It only brought out the worst in men, lying, cheating, and absolute denial of ma's natural need for variety in sexual companionships, of the opposite sex. Polygamy is a great host for truth, innocence, and youthful spirit is a bonus."

Frahmad spoke again, "I liked and needed to hear the part about maturity, as it relates to marriage.

Claude explained, "Age and maturity have nothing to do with each other. He laid heavy emphasis on the importance of maturity in holding a marriage together."

He had thought one was a factor of the other. He had to admit He was surprised to hear they are not codependent.

Frahmad shared Claude Anderson had explained, in a previous lecture, "Age merely relates or identifies the passage of time. For many the passage of time happens in a vacuum; they just get old. This is evidenced by stagnation in life pursuits and consistent repetitious and redundant acts on their parts. The example he gave was the following, "A baby is born. It comes into the world completely dependent and helpless. In time it learns to crawl. The crawling comes about as the baby pursues mobility and self-reliance. The baby who stops there stagnates. It doesn't learn to stand, walk, run, jump, hop, skip and so on. Yet, it ages;" he smiled. Then he continued, "The same baby who learns to stand, walk, run, etc; could be said to be maturing. Maturing is growing and accepting responsibility for a person's acts. In maturing flexibility in adapting into the roles required with ease is the measure."

In the same lecture, Claude made it clear that love and sex were in no way connected. "Sex is an exercise expressly engaged in by male and female couples to bring people into the life. Regardless of the outcomes, it is no way associated with Love. Sexual organs are reproductive organs.

They are not the love organs, by any means. "Claude told had them, in cases of rape by a person or persons previously unknown to the victim, love had no part in the act. It is not necessary to be in love to have sex. The business of prostitution requires lust to bring the John and the madam together. Love has nothing to do with it. There is no love between the prostitute and the john. These were some of the considerations taken in to account before the system opened its arms and welcomed polygamy. It solved problems of lying, deceiving, prostitution, infidelity, and rape. Homosexuality and unwanted children."

By now His room was a buzz of excitement as the things each person shared made clearer the wisdom in the decision to drop monogamy and embrace polygamy as the acceptable marriage.

He shared His feeling on the maturity built into polygamy. He contributed, "Marriage is the caring for the welfare of the entire person. Mature people only have sex to bring people into the world. Immature people have sex attempting to bind marital relationship together. Worst than that immature people have recreational sex. The result of this irresponsible and immature behavior too often is an unwanted child." In polygamous cultures all children are wanted. So the family to which the child is born is loved and cared for. In monogamous cultures these same children would somehow wind up in custody of the Public Assistance Services Department.

Mature people enter into the sexual act with the intent to bring a child into the world. Therefore, the act is approached in a different mindset. Both parties have as their goal adorning a new life with love and guidance. In the first instance, the intent is to host the ravages of lust. Children born in such a circumstance are unwanted. The highest function of sex is reproduction. The lowest function of sex is recreation. Under the old system of monogamy the percentage of children born yearly that were unwanted was outrageously high. Since the inception of polygamy few children were born that were unwanted. One thing became sobering clear, a marriage dependent upon lust was destined to fail and any children born of such a marriage might be damaged. Multiple partners prevented this from happening."

Frahmad said to the study group, "I like the way he delivered that. I believe that is the best way to end our project. What do you say?" The group agreed and talked on for hours. They ran over the two hours they had set for study and didn't know it.

Understanding the why of what they were living in made them feel powerful and fulfilled. Frahmad said, "I think we need to add the only time a man is able to have sex with one of his wives is when she is fertile and prime to bring a child into the world. While the females are free to have sex with any man at any time as long as the spouses knows about it. The males have the same privilege with females other than their spouses."

He said, "A good place to start our project will be the metaphor of 'the birds and bees.' We can explain why that metaphor is used."

Rhonda said, "I agree. It is a good starting point for a couple of reasons. First, birds and bees have sex, but they are not in love. It is an act-fostering perpetuation of the species. When a male bee has sex with a female bee, he doesn't profess love unending and devotion beyond description. It is simply an engagement of two of the same species endeavoring to reproduce and extend the existence of the species. It is done at a certain period of the year and when that period has passed it is no longer done until the time is again prime for reproduction. More important it needs to be said, so many people declare sex is the most important part of a marriage. It is not the most important part in a mature marriage."

"Caring for one another is the most important part of a mature marriage. Previously a major problem in the United States marriage was sex played too big of a part in relationships. Therefore the relationships were based on satisfaction of lusts and not fulfilling the need for love, humans have. A marriage without love is a marriage destined for failure. The best marriages happen among friends. They last. Lust will not bind a relationship. On the contrary, it will destroy it."

In certain advanced African cultures it was forbidden to have sex with anyone five years younger or older than yourself. Birds and Bees do not have sex with babies. Nor do birds and bees engage in same sex acts for love. Same sex acts and sex with children defiles the purpose of sex. These two abominations occur with great frequency in societies that have become insane. Make no mistake, homosexuality is not normal. It is an aberration.

Aberrations are not considered existence. They are forms of function. What do you think?" She said, as she ended, "Only, the terribly insane use children as masturbation objects and engage in same sex acts, or forced sexual acts." In a clamor of acceptance and approval they all stood, and embraced one another in acknowledgement.

After the ensuing class Claude congratulated them on their handling of a very touchy subject in a way that informed and not incensed the students. While their presentation was not a welcomed one by all, it left very little room for valid argumentation in opposition.

Chapter

9

SAFETY

"THE INSTANT A PERSON is conceived begins their exit from life. The safest way to live this experience is to be reADy to leave at a moments notice. No man or system can guarantee total safety. Doing the right thing is the safe way to live. Living daily in harmonious style is the advanced mode of living. That is the only safety to be found here. Securing oneself in "Do unto others as you would have them do unto you "is about as safe as you will ever be. Self-Mastery is the way to travel through this life. It was the highlighted portion of the New Education System. Today is your tomorrow. Be the best version of yourself everyday. Act now!"

"Those words were written on the air board in the History Classroom. Mr. Arumba Odebconda was the history teacher for His class. Arumba, Rumba the students called him, was a slight man in stature. Yet, with his dark skin and mild manner he stood taller than the highest hill. When he spoke his voice conveyed a quiet command of understandings. The man was a perfect match for the truths that flowed from his lip. No one ever slept through one of his classes. The man hAD the look. It was so intense that should students fall asleep his stare could wake them. The classmates all agreed his stare could penetrate closed eyelids. All of the students enjoyed laughing about his stare.

Arumba began, "History tells us what we did wrong. The lessons there inscribed have the power to direct our feet in more constructive directions. In the old system History was taught in the mode of Patriotism. The purpose of it being taught was to insure the people would without hesitation defend the way of life of the rich and powerful. What they were programmed to defend was different from what they were in truth defending. They were not securing better circumstances and conditions for their families. On the contrary, they were defending the rights of oppressors to continue to oppress their families and loved ones. Today we teach history with an aim of eliminating the oppressive conditions of the past."

He continued, "It was necessary to structure and end to War. A formula to end all wars was drawn. It held in its primary mandate the Declaration of all Lands Being Neutral. Also, Outlawing all Weapons, and the death Penalty for engaging in War, Colonization or Imperialistic endeavors as the most serious Crimes of all. Therefore the penalty was established as Execution, by garrotte. War and Human Oppression would no longer find life in the land. The rulers of the Dark World would no longer hold the hearts and souls of the innocent hostage as they ravaged the essence of all that is real."

"You will not be asked to remember dates and events, or heroes. You will be asked what methods do you believe will prevent negative events, related to dates, events and heroes from reacquiring." The idea is to think daily of actions that will bind us as a people and keep us from ever returning to any form of master and slave living. This is why we teach and this is why we learn. This is the gist of lessons in history today."

"Anthropological studies report money had made it possible for many inhumane acts to be carried-out. The manufacture of weapons was made possible by using money. War was possible by using money. Mass manipulation of humans was made possible using money."

Arumba continued, "The only life form that was forced to depend on money for necessities is Man. Under the guise of money making distribution of the common wealth fair people were brainwashed into believing money was assigned the role of equalizer. It was a great and purposeful lie. Its purpose was then, and would always be used to give advantage to evil idiocies. It is not real. In truth it has no value. Man kind had given it a value, and used it for their divers and dubious purposes. Money was the god of the evildoers. It was replaced with the Universal Stipend System."

"Throughout history there are constants that defy repudiations. Anthropological research proves such constants exist. To wit, 'All organizations are run for the benefit of the organizers, stands as one of these constants. No matter what the claim the group founding a movement or proposing to hold its actions as social improvements while collecting funds to operate, is hustling the people."

"Such an Organization was the International Standards Organization. It was heADquartered in Zurich, Switzerland. It regulated the value of currency around the world. Control of the value of currency gave a certain group control of the every day things in people's lives. Thus, Rule of the world was achieved by images, numbers on paper and coin in metals. After a while no one questioned the validity of the value of money, the necessity of its use, or what was being denied by its use. What the knight Templars sought to achieve was realized, control of the world by England. The World became deaf, dumb, and blind. A unique insanity took control of their sanity and they became mad. They sought pleasure, self-indulgence, substance abuse, raped women, and murdered their own species in wars both civil and private. The world was in one of the darkest periods ever. No other species sets about killing its own kind, unless it has gone mad. Money was behind it all."

"Even the black widow spider spares her male off springs."

"Money never could be useful, in truth. It had to go. It had to go because the group of warlocks, the Knights Templars, who contrived the use of it, did so to gain control of the World for King Richard III. Money had to go. Along with money Guns and Weapons had to go. Neither Money, nor Guns had ever proven to be instruments of safety."

The Council arrived at these conclusions after reviewing every Anthropological study available. All existing information revealed the same truth. "Any questions?" Rumba asked.

A hand waved feverishly in the middle of the class. Rumba said, "Stand and give us your name. I know who you are but your fellow students may not know you."

The person stood. Then said, "My name is Arrewphu. My question is simply this; we have emergencies in life when we need to get things done. How do we do that if we have no money or bank accounts?"

Arumba responded, "I see. You must be a new release from prison. Your question is well founded. Maybe you have not noticed we have competitive events and sports. Since no one in our day and time receives money for their contributions to our society, we have a Universal Stipend Fund in which points are allotted for just such cases. There is no red tape and the points may be used to relieve a situation, which is unmistakably identifiable as an emergency or as discretionary and disposable point credits or debits. The White plastic thing you were given upon your release form prison is the same as a charge card. It gets the job done." Don't hesitate to use the card for transactions in shops, stores, movie theatres, sporting events, and hospitals.

Arrewbu sat down.

Rumba, asked, "Any more questions?" The room was silent. A hand was raised in the front row. Rumba asked the young woman to stand and introduce herself to the class. The young woman rose and did as she was asked. "My name is Shereda Fountaine. My question is why do we need competition?"

Rumba walked from end to end of the lecture hall twice in silence, gazing at the floor. Standing in the left side of the hall words began to leap from his mouth. "We don't need competition with one another! As a whole body of people we need competition that is self-directed. Self directed competition drives one to improve their performance in the things they do.

"However, there are some among us who do need to compete with others. They should be able to do that. This level of competition is a dependent form of competition. Those who are caught in the throes of this competing are evaluating their worth against their ability to best someone else. Watching people compete is not harmful to the spectator in anyway. So it was concluded that it would be a part of the new system. The feats of the competitors would be recorded and documented for proving their acclaim to exceptional performances, only. There would be no money involved in anyway with these competitions, just glory."

Rumba smiled and said, "We will conclude this segment on safety by a short story. A Brahma Bull was leading his baby bull son across some railroad tracks. He noticed his son hAD gotten his tail caught in the railroad ties. Attempting to set himself free, the baby bull was trying to bite his tail to free himself. The senior bull noticed a train coming. He politely told the young bull, "Son never lose your head over a little piece of tail. Safety is best achieved by Self-Mastery. Any time anybody or anything risks biting a piece of tail, it may cost them the loss of their head's."

"Safety is always in your hands. Living right is a thing we all need to focus on. Living right neutralizes fear of harm from others or leaving life. Doing the right thing will ever produce an unconquerable people. Even though others may conquer the land, they have accomplished little should they fail to conquer the will of the people. That is your safety without dependence on fire arms and weapons."

Chapter

10

QUALITY IN QUALITY OUT

MILDRED LANDRY STOOD AS the most prolific Professor of Sociography of her time. She spent twenty-six years among indigenous communities existing far from the reaches of either Western Ideology or Modern thought. Her lectures focused on Socio-psychographic in Human Development. Basically stated, environment produces people. Her research reveled people who are living outside of time are alive. Living outside of time, as they do, there is no thought involved in their lives. Living outside of time they are responsive to all that is alive. That responsiveness is absolute being, is her stand. A part from being a Master Teacher, she was praised by her peers for credibility of her research and its irrefutability. More of her students were advancing the cause of Social Development and Reforms than any other teachers'.

Numerous independent Governments funded longitudinal studies to discredit her findings. They came up short. The task was relegated to the United Nations to disprove her study, as well as her books on the subject. All of their combined efforts and resources proved faint in disproving her conclusions and solutions.

As she walked into the room she began speaking.

"Since there is nothing new under the Sun, I vouch safely the following adage of the Ancients. "The only indicator of human advancement is how well we are getting along together and how well we are taking care of one another." Taking care of one another was impossible under the Witch Craft of the illuminati, the elite, the Bilderberg group, the Shiners, Skull and bones, and the masons, and other secret brotherhood and sisterhoods. These organizations and others similar to them have used the life experience as their playpen. Overtime they have demonstrated they are sociologically anti the survival of the human race. Their root principles are evil and left unchecked through they technology will destroy the world. They are mad men and claim supremacy over all. Fact is they are Warlocks and Witches who are masters of the dark arts. While sitting on their butts they drive people to compete with one another for their entitlements."

"People driven to compete for basics and needs, generally, are precursory social conditions leading to the destruction of the system under which they have lived and suffered. Competition has its place. It is instrumental and food the human experience when competing with self. It is a debilitating factor when it is dependent of besting others. Some systems engage in pitting its people against each other are lingering in Self Destruct mode. The system itself becomes the most aggressive terrorist it will come across. The deterioration of the old system had many Achilles heels. None was more suspect for its decline than the lack of pride in the things that were produced. When people lose themselves, due to external factors, their regard for making good contributions to their communities dies. It is a reasonable outgrowth of meaningless existence. Life makes no sense to them so why invest your efforts beyond tokenism. They decline downward in producing quality products, proficiency in management is unheard of, and people do little as possible for as much money as possible. Pride in what they produce is not the motivating factor. The motivating factor is they have bills to pay."

"There is no spiritual or scientific connections with the Job beyond they are able to pay their bills. Labor that is detached from being meaningful to self-development is Slavery."

"When quality is lacking in products produced in a community, the door is left open for better products to enter the market. A natural result is jobs for the people in the community disappear and the economy collapses. Other institutions crumble and fall in a domino effect and finally the **traditional family** lies smoldering in rubble. These are a few of the characteristic of a system that has, as is citizens, people who have no regard for competing with themselves, so they may improve. The major travesty of the above is systems such as that destroys the family."

"By structuring a system that included the acceptability of destruction of the family, as inconsequential, the Illuminati and the Elite cut their own throats. Their objective was to fashion a productive creature that would operate robotically. It did not happen. They lost their labor force. Low quality people were the overall result. The most important institution in any society or community is the family. It provides people to fill the gaps left by departing elders of the community. Naturally, the quality of people a community produces depends on the strength of the family and the stability it affords its youths. It is impossible for the family to produce quality people when both parents spend the major portion of their day laboring at the discretion of others, and focusing on food, clothing, and shelter. Instead of being preoccupied with parenting, the adults are mired in the muck involved in securing basic human entitlements, for their families. It leaves the youths faced with shadowy images of ghosts stumbling through routines of fragmented roles into dysfunctional. Quality youths will be lost to alcohol addiction, promiscuity, homosexuality, immoral acts and substance abuse. The result, generally, quality people vanish and the society dies. The youth's aspirations descend to the lower levels of self-expectation the system has deviously devised for them. In systems such as that quality people are not required. Robotic people serve better."

"Robotic people follow a specific pre-programmed script. They are unable to be flexible or modify their actions. Their lives are somnambulistic. They are as sleep walkers. As people woke up they began to stray from the script and modify their roles. The change in their behavior marshaled in the change of social role play. Role play is the fundamental component in human social relation development and child development as well.

Each transition must accompany adjustments in a person's actions. The transition from single to married requires changes in role play. The transition from husband to father requires modifications in role play.

When roles are undefined and gender looses its identity cultures find it difficult, if not impossible, to produce quality people. Even roles have to be adaptive towards the objective of developing wholesome communities. Then women find no reason to be men and vice a versa. They find it unnatural to step out of gender and assume reverse gender roles. It is unnatural. Humans are the only life form that explains it as normal. It is a learned behavior, and a gross departure from reality. God in his almighty grace and wisdom aids the misguided individuals in their misguided journey with reinforcements and supports. God guides those who seek right guidance and those who seek misguidance equally. God does not discriminate. A person makes a choice and God supplies whatever is needed to realize the choice. That does not always constitute Reality. It is merely that age-old demon at work, form of function. Merely being able to perform in a certain way doesn't necessarily constitute reality. When people deny what they were created to be, God in no way interferes. It is person's right to choose and God's undeniable pleasure to supply what the person has chosen, proper or improper. In the end God stands in Judgment a person's choices. That is the danger of free will power, which man has and no other creature has. Many people making poor choices may lead some people to join in errant choices resulting in a decline in the quality of people in a culture."

"People of a community need to be quality or aspire to be products of quality. It is no easy task. In the old System role strain had gotten out of control. People felt it was proper to do whatever they wanted to do. It was determined by the Council the behavior did not coincide with reality. It was a form of function. Role strain occurs most frequently when people in a community attempt to make too much out of life. They take it too seriously. Due to role strain they stray form being cast in a role amenable for family perpetuation and become adept in practicing conflicting roles. The role conflict by its nature reduces need for quality people. All the old system sought was bodies to fill slots in its dark plan. It had no regard for sanity."

"Unless people are dedicated to the improvement and the development of their species they will continue to deny the danger of deviant practices that produce low quality people. People of low origin in conception can hardly be expected to fit the demands of the roles needed to guide a community's youths to themselves. These were the conclusions of the Council. It meant sacrificing a few to save the many, so be it."

"The content of this lecture is not fitted to your knowledge, wisdom, reason, logic, or computation, it is through understanding that the traveler will find the gifts contained here."

Mildred walked to the podium, opened a bottle of water, drank deeply and said, "I will expect no less than ten questions from each of you before our next meeting, which will be two days from now. Please make sure you have your name, zotgram address, and student identification numbers on your questionnaire. Normally, I provide answers to my students' questionnaires in two class days. However, it may take longer for me to get to all of you, as I have been led to understand some of you are very smart and may ask difficult questions, the class size is extra large, and some questions may require investigational conformation, before delivering a truthful response, My zotgram address is on the air board, Class dismissed!"

Mildred's classes were always short and succinct. Generally, most of the students remained in the class after it ended. She enjoyed chatting openly with them and it allowed them to compare notes. The main idea behind them staying was to work together to consciously live better together. The healing messages mean absolutely nothing if not given the due diligence of practice, practice. Practice!

Chapter

11

GOVERNMENT

CHARLOTTE HENSON IS A Professor of Socio-economics. She spoke with an awakening frankness as she entered the room. "There is but one clear and discernable indicator of human progress and spiritual amalgamation. It is how well we are getting along together and how well we are taking care of each other. All forms of imposed Government are false. When Man is sane and being Himself he has himself under his control. When Man is himself, he has no need for external governing."

Then she said, "I know you've heard it before." She smiled and said, "I bet you haven't heard this one. 'That government which governs least, governs best'. Supposedly, people elect public officials to lookout for their interests. In reality Big Government looks out for its own interests and those of the Rich. It is their Country the soldier protects. In truth, the soldier has no Country."

She continued, "Big Government's aim is to rule the many for the benefit of the few. There is no reason to fund a study to prove that fact. A less than casual perusal of World History will scrawl that message across the forehead of most people."

She said, "All organizations are run for the benefit of the organizers." That is reality. The only society existing under complete liberation is a society populated with people who have united in self-mastery. Masters of self are no problem to the world, neither are they trouble by the world."

"It is ironic the only agent that can guarantee your total liberation is God. Until Man escape fear of others, he will not know Liberation and true safety. Fearing the wrath of God is good. Loving God is better. Through the loving of God it is possible to attain liberation. It is by loving God that we favor our brothers and sisters. It is by loving God that Man welcomes his reunion with God. Humans who attend to self-mastery need no external Governing entity. They live inside themselves and the outer world holds neither consequence nor reward for them. They are masters of self and require no exterior governing. Humans existing at this level will peacefully resist compliance with any forced conditions."

"Formal Governments have always and will ever stand as Agents for ruling and oppressing domineering classes. It is they who fear the rule of other men. They know the nature of mongrels that strive to control others, for their personal gains. Who ruled, throughout the ages, has mattered little to the brainwashed who funded Governments of yesteryear. Their lives were not affected for the better by the change in Masters. It has always been the old rulers whose lives were affected."

The ruled just get pushed around by a new group of parasites. The rulers fund their desires and leisure at the expense of the ruled. The people fund their oppression with taxes, obeying, and sacrificing their children to wars to gain wealth, and worldly power, for their rulers. The rulers find ways to avoid taxes and belligerently press the ruled for more taxes. This is made possible by an indigent human processing that miss educates humans. The processing makes the distasteful, palatable. No organization or Government holds within its basic components social development or social welfare. Formal Government operates best when it is exploiting the Governed.

Exploitation deprives people of social development. A Community, Society, Nation, or the World can in no way attain to liberation unless the major portions of its people are self-masters. A society with masters of self is a society of developing people. They will not yield to oppression."

"Conclusions for directing man's steps in the way of human development, for the future, were derived through thorough study of the past. It was deemed fair and necessary to critically examine the operation of several branches of Government to demonstrate the primary concerns of government were securing the positions of the rulers, and preserving its self. Examining the Old Justice Department will do for starters."

"The Old Justice Department offers an opportunity to see its true function. It was a formal branch of Government which was clearly one of the most inappropriately named agencies in the Chronicles of Human advancement."

"It functioned like this in adjudication of the common mans' affairs. A burglar breaks into a home. In so doing the burglar is first, guilty of trespassing, invasion of privacy, as well as burglary with intent to kill, provided the resident is in the house and asleep. The owner of the home shoots him and wounds him seriously. The priority for the Justice System is the rights of the burglar. The burglar, by law, has the right to sue the homeowner. His civil rights have been violated. In California it is legal for the burglar to sue the homeowner. It is against the law to defend yourself. That is a joke. When the burglar decided to enter the home of the victims his civil rights were no longer valid. That would be justice.

Before shooting the burglar the two struggle and the homeowner receives multiple wounds. The burglar receives medical care at the expense of the citizens. The homeowner has to cover his own medical expenses. The burglar gets free medical care. When the burglar recovers from his wounds, he is put on trial. Taxpayers cover the cost of the trial including the cost of his defense attorney. They pay everybody, the judge, the court recorder, the district Attorney, the bailiff, the public defender, the police officers, the psychiatrist, psychologist, the probation officer, and the jury. The victim has to get his home fixed through his insurance company, or out of pocket. He finds himself in a catch twenty-two. Doing the repairs out of pocket sets him back financially. Turning in a claim to his insurance company will net him an increase in his premiums. Either way he is screwed. The burglar on the other hand, wins no matter which way it goes. A verdict of guilty would've remanded him to a situation where he got three hots and a cot. A verdict of not guilty will release him to prey upon more people. There were satellite components that benefited from the burglar's judicial sanctity; private alarms systems, homeowner's insurance, security doors windows, and fences. These entities also dug deeply into the citizens' pockets and depended on the perpetuation of crime. None of the above wanted crime to go away, except the home owner."

"It does not require a mathematical genius to see the egregious amount of money pumped into the economy by the justice system partnering with crime. It was a clever way to build the economy and control the continued generation of cash flow. The Justice Department was dependent upon crime. The existence of crime guaranteed jobs for those who had jobs directly related to criminal dispensations as well as those who had casual relationships with crime. Crime and Justice were locked in a symbiotic waltz of two sanguine parasites satisfying their dependency, at the expense of the general citizenry."

"What was most revealing, for the eye of candor, was the true victims in this farce were the citizens. The council of Elders viewed the Justice System through unbiased spectacles. It found the system had more holes in it than a ten-foot board of wormwood. It was providing anything but solutions to the problems. It had to go. It took three years to devise and implement a better method. It was tested in five areas and the results were supportive of the Councils' approval and conclusion. Then it was approved for worldwide implementation. Personnel who earned money through the Old Justice System were assigned other works."

"Similarly, the Council scrutinized the elected officials and found the entire process ludicrous. The people were paying people to deny them what they were entitled to have as birthrights. Meanwhile, the elected officials were living extravagant lives. Some had three or more homes that cost in the millions. Others had homes in several states. These homes were fully furnished and In most cases the elected officials had business managers to oversee the staffs employed in these opulent homes. The maintenance on these homes could run up as high as $ 150,000.00 per year. The elected officials had medical insurance and received pensions upon retiring that would allow them to live very well into their declining years."

"In the midst of the affluent life-styles of the elected Representatives and members of Congress too many of the people who were paying them to administer their affairs, were struggling to eke out a life-style below the poverty line. Others were sleeping under newspaper on city streets, Bus stations, living in cardboard boxes, finding shelter under bridges and going hungry. Meanwhile the elected officials were living the great life. Historically they had gotten fat from the way they miss-managed the electorate's affairs. The brainwash the people were exposed to, more aptly known as 'Miss education, had them believing that was reality; the best they could get or expect. It was the best Deal in town! It was a lie. What was happening was Criminal in covert and clandestine senses. Sure it was Government with two distinct parties, but they both were corrupt and legislated in the best interest of their constituencies, the rulers. In essence it was a one party system."

"Both Parties functioned in the interests of the Rich and the Power Mongers. Government allocated funds, generated by the people, to exploration of space. The money spent on that Colonization procedure would've been best spent on providing, moderate shelter for all Americans, medical for all Americans, and other human entitlements to All Americans. Instead billions were wasted on the "space race" by both Parties." Government was spitting in the people's faces at every turn.

"This insult was extremely apparent in the attitude of the Bureau of Alcohol, Fire Arms, and Tobacco. These things generated unimaginable amounts of money for the treasury of the Nation. Although all three were extremely detrimental to the health and welfare of the people, the law kept them legal."

"Alcohol was a bad drug. People would get drunk and drive cars. The number of people killed in accidents related to alcohol was staggering. Equally unacceptable was the number of people killed in fights, brawls, and domestic violence where alcohol was involved. Despite the number of deaths directly connected to alcohol; it remained legal. It was a fantastic source for cash flow. It was addictive and repeat sales were a certainty. Yes, the Bureau knew it was both addictive and lethal. The taxes it generated made the loss of human life and the physically addictive nature of alcohol pardonable. There were many excuses and justification vouchsafed to keep it legal. Not one of the excuses was self-validating. One justification was, if we make it illegal bootleggers would start up again. Government had the resources to not only shut them down, but also make it hazardous to their health to disregard it being sold. Government had the Rule Book.

"In the 1970's a group became active in support of better education in the African-American Communities. The group was labeled subversives, by the government, and an all out attack was launched to eradicate it. The mission of the group was to raise the standard of the African American living conditions through community Development Programs without violence. Within two years the government wiped it off the face of the Earth. Similarly, the Ku Klux Klan has been involved in subversive and un-American activities for over two hundred years and the government had been unable to do a thing about them. Any fodder the elected officials could muster pales in light of circumstances such as this. Another bogus excuse was keeping it legal we can control the quality of it and make sure nothing is sold that is either a danger to the eyes or distilled under unsanitary conditions, hog wash. Alcohol kills thirty thousand brain cells per minute. Brain cells are the only cells in the body that do not reproduce. They gave many similar reasons why it should remain legal. Truth is they needed the tax revenue to run their con game. It all amounted to making something legal that really needed to be illegal. The concern of the bureau was the generation of revenue. There was zero concern with the welfare of the public. People were plentiful and expendable. The fact that they got drunk and drove cars, shot one an other was irrelevant."

"In keeping with this tendency of Government to look out for special interest and disregard the people, were fire arms. First, no groups should have the authority to use firearms. Protectors of the peace need firearms in extreme circumstances. Fire Arms should not be big business. Hunting with firearms was replaced with bow and arrow hunting. Those in the firearms business promoted the idea that having a gun in the home would ensure a degree of safety for the family, not so. An improved Justice system was the remedy for that social problem. Just how safe were you when your shooting a burglar attempting to enter your home landed you in jail. Legally the burglar could have you arrested for attempted murder, and you might find yourself sentenced to ten to twenty-five years in prison. The laws on the use of firearms were sketchy, as they pertained to the legal use in the hands of citizens, but heavily weighted in the favor of the criminal in bends and twists of legal applications. From this brief example it is easy to see the conundrum posed by the impugned stated purpose of firearms and the working principles of their use in the old system. Unmasked it was apparent that it was all about the money and not the welfare of the citizens."

"Given what is known about Tobacco, it was a waste of time to make a credible case for its positive contributions to the human experience. Of all the merciless things mankind had done to man in demonstrating his distain for man, the production and sale of tobacco products stood a top the list. For years government had known tobacco was taking lives at a rate to large to keep accurate data on. They hid the damaging effects of cigarette smoking by the invention of diseases. One of them was called Consumption. The symptoms were black lungs that were partially eaten away. Later they called it Black Lung Disease. It was Lung Cancer. Cigarettes were a big cash flow item for the Government in taxes and cash flow for the Tobacco Industry. It was safely estimated two hundred percent of the price of a pack of cigarettes was tax. The big problem with cigarettes was getting a person to smoke that first one. It was a certainty that nicotine would do the rest. To accomplish the job of getting that first one between a person's lips the aid of the psychologist was enlisted. Advertising the products was turned over to them and they did a grand job of turning an unsuspecting society into a society of tobacco addicts. The Government was making money and the tobacco manufactures were making profits, and the people were dying. Neither the Government, nor the Tobacco Industry gave a kitty. The people were a means towards and ends, and no more. Tobacco was a major contributor to the task which lie before the Government, 'Manifest the Destiny outlined by the original invaders of North America. Do this as a first and only priority even if it meant the death of every man, woman, and child sustain the witchcraft though it be dark and murky as the silt of the mighty Mississippi River."

73

"It was unquestionably Witch Craft. Any form of human manipulation for a group or personal benefit is Witch Craft."

"Management of these branches of Government was under the control of the ruling class. The rulers were outrageously remise in their responsibility and loyalty to the people. Government claimed it was designed to, operated for the welfare of its citizens. That was a lie. It functioned in a mode that resembled a direct contradiction to its proposed mission."

"These three examples were enough in themselves to warrant the Elders decision to phase Government out. All Formal forms of Government were phased out. Self-mastery was adopted as a major portion of holistic education, and human development."

"Government was replaced with self-mastery. Without exception everyone was held accountable for his or her actions. Human education focused on being responsible for ones actions as part of a whole. People were trained to see themselves in all that exists and learned how to see all as associative parts of the ONE self. No longer were humans instructed for the fulfillment of slots prepared by the slavers. Education had as its ends harmony with all things animate and inanimate. It further embraced a thorough immersion into those things intangible yet, everlasting as the greater part of SELF. In self-mastery all is seen as self, and self is seen as all that is, seen or unseen. This change facilitated richer lives and over a ten year period removed crime completely from the face of the Human Culture."

"The justice system was replaced with three person panels. Individuals were selected from the population to hear and resolve conflicts and dilemmas. The panel listened to all evidence and witnesses relating to the situation, and its decision was final. There were no attorneys and the system of legal mumble jumble was scrapped. The codes for crimes were explicit and the resolves were carried-out in two days. There were no prisons."

"Finally, Tobacco, Alcohol, and Fire Arms were declared illegal. There was a zero tolerance for possession of any of the above. They were cloistered under the grouping of astringent Witch Craft facilitators, and band forever."

Charlotte pauses for a moment. Then, she say's, "Our next meeting will be at the beach. It will be byor. The session will start at the regular time and end at the regular time. What you do afterwards is your own business. However, you are expected to bring two solutions to past events associated with this session. To prevent the past errors from reoccurring we must practice deterring them and adopting new and better strategies of occluding them. By examining clarity of the information we may sort out the factual from the fictional. In every age and every time henceforth, we need to live the Real. Your questions are vital to the continued survival and prosperity our species."

"Before we end this session it is important to remember, miss education did not occur at the hands of the teachers. They were merely following the mandates and dictates of the educational system."

"Thank you very much for your attention and see you at the beach!"

She smiled and glided from the room.

Chapter

12

THE GOAL

HUMANS ENTER THIS JOURNEY as infants. The next step of development is children. It is closely followed by adolescence. Which leads to teenager and is the onset of young adulthood. Young adulthood folds into adulthood then a person is able to fend for himself or herself Successfully. These transitions occur in life without much effort and will be experienced by people in varying degrees of lucidity. The difficult transition to make is the final transition that requires effort, Maturity. The transitions that precede maturity happen with the passing of time. Maturity is different.

In maturity the discordant habits people acquire over time must bow to proper self-government. The Mature person does what is the best thing to do among choices.

A fit person is better able to host maturity than an unfit person. A person who is physically fit is most likely mentally fit, also. Physical fitness is linked to mental acuity, to some degree. There are no absolutes in life. However, fit people have demonstrated the ability to control themselves and make reasonably good choices.

The mature person is ever growing and seeking greater understands of being. In this search for improved being the mature person is always searching for ways to improve the experience of living by being a compliment to Creation. The immature person is ever in search of ways to exploit people and the Creation. They have a name for it, "Progress." Most of them are physically fit, but unfit in morals and character.

Physical fitness is an on going individual responsibility. Each course mandated that students attend off campus locations for fitness training. Charlotte's class meeting at the Beach was routine. Training involved warm-up, exercises, and games. He understood the importance of the games and relished the biweekly sessions at the beach. The intent of the games was to perform maintenance of the body. Some of the games developed the eye hand coordination. Other games pursued agility and elasticity. There were multiple games for endurance and balance. Still other games were for mental focus and centering oneself. At the end of the sessions the energy levels of all of them were high and so renewing. They were encouraged to workout on their own, but you know how that goes. The mature had regular schedules for self-maintenance. The immature found many reasons why they did not have enough time to FIT . . . it into their lives. Most of them did little to follow up the beach sessions. However, as time passed the number of those actively finding time for exercise grew. When the session was over Charlotte found a quiet spot and threw herself in the sand. She rested for a moment. Then she ran walked to warm down.

The States during reconstruction had found it a good idea to apportion some beaches as school locations and granted the schools exclusive privilege during specified hours. As a trade off the schools were responsible for the care and maintenance of those areas e.g. Maintenance of some Beaches, Bird Sanctuaries, Parks, and other areas dependent upon Man's connecting with his larger self, the environment. The world was becoming beautiful and Man was seeing it as himself as in days gone by. The blindness that had rendered his eyes useless peep holes hAD become passages for life and the world around Man was being seen for what it was, self.

After the beach He, Sheila, and Frahmad stopped for refreshments and salad. He said, "So far I have gained from these General Studies and Classes, the reason we have had Governments in the past is because we had been unable to govern ourselves properly. In so doing we left it open for cunning and unscrupulous individuals to capitalize on this social discrepancy in human development. Is that how you see it?"

Sheila started laughing and slamming the table top with the palms of her hands; Frahmad began laughing too, and told Sheila, "Girl control yourself"!

Sheila stopped laughing shortly after that and began a polite conversation starting with, "Have you any idea how much power you have as an individual and we as a collective?" She continued, "We are the masters of our fate. We are what we have been in search of. We determine what will be and what will not be. The turnings and twisting of fate and destiny occur either through action or inaction, by the people. We are the power. The action that is most effective is self-control. Through self-control it is possible to realize Reality. In the past we were ignorant of this truth and robbed and denied access to our ultimate success in this temporary journey, union with our source, God. We were led to believe fallacious lies. Lies such as there is no after life, and we should do whatever, in quiet desperation." Before she could finish Frahmad interrupted her.

Frahmad chimed in, "It is not easy to remain focused. Life is full of distractions. It is for this reason we attend these sessions. We must do everything we can to prevent the past disgrace to the human experience from ever happening again. As long as we practice our roles and rehearse them until forever begins and never, never come no more we have command of preventing the socially inhumane tragedies of the past. We must be fully able to forgive, but not forget. It is in forgetting that we allow devious miscreants to obstruct our paths, to construct laws that enslave the masses, and extends privileges to them. Among us at any time there are rascals who wait in abeyance to construct cages without sides to restrain the people and grant obstreperous liberties to them. The training makes us ever mindful of the presences that prowl among us with deceit and consternation as its constant vanguard. It never sleeps."

He said. "On the surface the travesty of the past seems necessary and proper. However, as I look further into the content of what had been uncovered in these sessions I must admit without equivocation, there is truth in the lectures. I am still out on concluding the events of the past were necessary. What was before was blatant Witch Craft. It just should not have happened."

He was sitting on the edge of his chair; he paused and sat back in his chair, scratched his head with his right hand and glanced down to his right and continued. "It took great temperance to uncover the reality of the system enslaving the people, it claimed it protected. Many people faced hardships and indignities to expose it for what it was. Even today there those among us some who deny it was improper to do what the slavers did. They pretend it would have met with their approval had the traffickers in slavery made slaves of them; we know that is a lie. The system controlled the every day lives of everybody in the entire World by using money. It is easy to dupe people. People will believe a lie before they will believe the truth. In shrewd and diabolical manipulations the pedants convinced the people money had power. Ensuring those things did not happen again was vital."

"Money had no more power than blank paper. It was the force behind the paper that empowered the paper, the gun and the justice system. The rulers of the World concocted the paper system and endowed it with value. They controlled the rulebook. It did not bother them that the game they were running was a crooked game. In the end the final analysts proved the system depended on the people being out of self-control, totally abandoning responsibility, and totally abnegating self-mastery. Those conditions were perfect for that sophisticated brand of slavery to be imposed on the people. There was adequate evidence to support two extremely important conclusions, primarily the use of money-inhibited freedom. Lastly, money was a chain, a control device. The wide spread of Self-Mastery that ensued throughout the World neutralized the Rule Book."

Frahmad and Sheila exclaimed in unison, "Yes, yes, yes!""

Sheila said, "The sessions are not a brain wash as has been circulated by those who will tell any lie to return to the old ways. For us to remain watchful we must be reminded of the past."

He said, "I know that now. I even know how little the good life held for the rich. They were miserable!"

A silence followed His remarks. Although they were full of vigor it was channeled into radiating light. They glowed with the luminescence of unity with all that is. The meal was finished in that environment of quiet and silence. They left the restaurant He and Sheila walked together. Frahmad headed in the direction of Downtown.

The sky was clear and night's curtain was rapidly surrounding them. In an hour or so it would be dark. The dark ebbed closer and the dark blue canopy above summoned and coaxed the heavenly bodies to shed their shyness and light the blue-black velvet night canopy. It was spring and easy for one heart to envelope itself in another heart. They walked as if in a dream. Possibilities for real family, real devotion, and real growth were in the trees, the air, especially in them, and everywhere. The fragrances of grass and flowers were things of cleansing. One of the features of the new education was they had learned how to step outside of time. It was part of the core course of self-mastery. It also included how to consciously step out of their bodies for extended periods. These things as well as greater awarenesses of who they were became classified as normal human being.

Sri Keyan Kenyananata was the primary instructor for the Yoga and Spiritual Alchemy Classes. He taught there are no limits. There is just learning. Everything was filled with vibrating life, yet stilled by a notion that could only be understood in the unification of everything transcending into unison. The basis for all of his lectures was founded on one principle idea, "I am That."

High above the stars began to twinkle one by one until the heavens were a glow with a billion lights. Stars were twinkling and blinking in a symphony of light that was spell binding. The vastness of the spectacular universe engulfed them in its harmony and they would after be new. They were neither on Earth, nor any tangible station. For the very first time in His life He felt unrestricted. It was the greatest rush of His life. He knew, for the first time what it felt lie to be alive, but yet not fully alive.

Chapter

13

HEALING TIME

HE AND SHEILA HAD become close companions. So, they decided to vacation together that year. Each year all adults earned a four-week vacation to anywhere in the world. If they limited the vacation to places in the territory they lived in it could be extended to eight weeks. Either way all expenses were paid for the vacation.

That year they decided it would be Brazil. From Brazil they could go to Venezuela or Uruguay with ease. Neither of them spoke Brazilian Portuguese. Nevertheless the lure of the lush greenery and limpid blue waters beckoned 'come to me and drink in my nectar.' They were extremely excited and hurriedly arranged their affairs for the trip. Rio Grande do Sul, Brazil was their final destination. It was filled with the excitement of South America without the bluster of the more commercialized cities. It promised the undaunted glamour of the big city and the all embracing irresolute romance and intrigue of the Jungle.

The flight to Brazil was mainly over water. It offered an opportunity to put some things in proper perspective. Looking out the window at the Majestic Splendor of the Pacific Ocean below and the vast open spaces of the infinite sky above made Him and Her aware of their importance in the scheme of things. The vastness of the

Pacific Ocean and the infinite reaches of the sky bonded them one to the other and the importance of being master of self as uniquely the unifying and harmonizing factors. What, if anything, is important, made Him question His existence.

The materially wealthy had been in no better stead than the poor. This was obvious now. They moved about in squalor of the filth and depravity of self-deception. All the money in the world could not have improved their state of self-satisfaction. They were spiritually impoverished. Their aims and objectives had bound them in a different type of Ghetto. All they knew how to do was make money. Sadly, they were convinced there was nothing after life. This talent for conjuring riches had blinded them to reality. The primary content of the life-style they sought and ever clung to was a lazy self-indulgent life.

They sought leisure. They had become so insane that they believed leisure and pleasure were the total content of living. Many of them had become mad; they were having sex with their own infants and daughters. It never dawned on them they were caught in an enormous trap. Generation after generation had fallen victim to the trap's lure. Empires had crumbled and fallen under its crooked and gnarled hand. Now it had a new group of unsuspecting victims. No matter how attractive it looked outside, it lacked spiritual supplication and beauty inside. A person reliant on others to earn their daily bread is in error. Pursuing fake reality, a big rattrap, had victimized them.

His mind went to a time and place He enjoyed, before the death of His father. His father's eldest brother owned a candle and coffee shop. It was a place to go light a candle and sip coffee. It was strange how quiet it always was in the shop. The candles were scented and the teas were from around the world. It wasn't lavish by any standard; it was comfortable and peaceful. No matter the time of day people were always there. It was a climate where people felt one another instead of chattering. In the awesome quiet they could connect without speaking, and it was good. His uncle played avant-garde recordings so softly, they could hardly be heard. The lighting in the shop was all candlelight except the natural light from the front windows. The colors were soft and flowed into each in unity. Conversation was light and people spent the majority of their time watching the flames of the candles dance. The quiet movement of the flickering flames soothed the ravages of the daily encounters with worldly nonsense.

There were tables and chairs for the guests. Each table had a scented candle in the center. There were eight chandeliers that held candles. The chandeliers were styled early Egyptian and added a touch of antiquity to the decorum.

He was old. Every now and then he would tell a story. No, it wasn't a story it was a fable or folklore. On this day the subjects of fame, fortune, and being rich came up.

He chuckled and started moving his head shaking it from side to side, as if he was losing it. He looked up and around and a silence fell over the shop. His gaze touched the eyes of every person's eyes in the shop.

Into that stillness He spoke, "Oh several years ago, must've been at least twenty, a neighbor had a fruit orchard."

"Now, in this orchard there was one tree that produced the most delicious fruit of all the trees in that orchard. It did not produce enough for him to sell vast quantities and provide a better life-style for his family. Nor could he offer any portion of its fruits without his patrons wanting those fruits, only. He would lose business were he to let anyone know how delicious the fruit from that tree was. The law of supply and demand being what it is he was prohibited from letting any one knowing about the fruit."

"In time one of the branches on that tree decided it would produce a piece of fruit that would be the most exceptional piece of fruit on the tree. Soon after the other fruits on that tree began to shrivel and sour. They became bitter and tasteless. The one piece of fruit was consuming the best substance from the tree. Before long the withering of the other branches of that tree foretold of its unhealthy state. Where there had been deeply vividly green leaves there now were pale green leaves and light tan leaves hesitantly clinging to a tree that was once healthy and filled with life. The previously, dark brown trunk of that tree was now a pale ash brown. Its bark was peeling and sap was oozing from its exposed roots. One year the fruit blossoms did not favor that tree. That tree struggling to survive began to draw sustenance from the trees around it. As time passed it was apparent the repeated producing of this one delicious piece of fruit was killing the orchard. Came the day it was the only tree left in the orchard."

"Although it was the only tree remaining in the orchard, it was a shadow of itself. It no longer produced the one piece of delicious fruit. It stood alone barren and offered not even nest to bird, squirrel, or insect."

He held his right hand high, tossed a kiss to all with his left hand, turned and continued his journey through the shop.

Such is the nature of false realities, greed, and institutionalized slavery. They ravage everything near first and devour all that is far eventually. Imperialism victimizes everybody. The agent of the slavery is no freer than his captives. He must guard them and fear them. The control obtained by this type of life style pales in desirability with the light of Truth and sucks the life out of everything.

For among the pinions of leisure time lays mere self- discontentment than self-appreciation. Idle time had victimized them more than the poverty they created for the financially indigent. With portended virtue as their banner the wealthy and rich found infidelity appealing and sought the spouses of friends to consort with and fed the veracious appetites of divers abominations. Their life progress ends at drug abuse, infidelity, gambling, substance abuse, vices, addictions, child molestation, rape, and prostitution, etc. They organized elaborate orgies and lust flaunted itself in grand style. The acts did nothing more than create a larger void in their already empty lives.

This led many of them to using children for objects conducive to masturbation, only. At some point the quest led to soliciting young children in other cultures. Affluent and well to do males were trying to find wholesomeness in sexual acts with girls and boys five years of age to thirteen years of age. The older children did not deliver the same gratification as the young children did, for them. Their spiritual leaders and priest heard their confessions, and then went into sinful acts against the children of their progeny, themselves. Trusted and ordained Catholic Priests, who had taken a vow of celibacy, were molesting children. All the while the Church knew it was going on and had the temerity to look away. They hid it. The inequality they affected by their disproportional dispersion of the Common Wealth of the Earth proved grossly deficient in reciprocity. At last the insanity caused by their self-deception awoke the demon of homosexuality. Historically, the in rise homosexual relations and the disintegration of Formal and Organized Religion signal the death of a Culture.

He came to the conclusion the thing that was of greatest importance in this experience was Self Mastery. It was the one thing that was absolutely doable. All else was surrounded by circumstance and external dependency. In the past many had opted to abuse others rather than master-self. It was a lot easier to control others than to control self. The only requirement for controlling others was to have no self-control. Every one of the above actions stood as examples of what happens when people are deficient in self-control. It is a gross mistake to assume at any point or time in the life experience doing 'whatever' is okay. It just isn't so. It leads to misery for all.

Several hours had passed before they could see the water giving way to the lush green foliage of Brazil. They landed at SalgADo Filho Airport. They would stay In Rio Grande do sol for three weeks and travel by boat to Rio de Janeiro for four weeks. A week before departing Brazil they would return to Rio Grande do Sol. Neither of them had had a vacation in two years. The extra two weeks was approved by the Central Agency of Vacations.

Processing through Customs was lengthy; two hours after landing and deplaning they were at their lodgings. By the standards of the time their accommodations were five star.

Few hotels on the planet equal the splendor of Varanda Das Bromelisa Boutiques. It was on a par with latter day five star hotels. Those accommodations were available and the common vacation places for people. Vacationers also hAD the option of living with local people. Either way there was no charge. Man no longer used his home as an anchor. It was now a sail.

Its accommodations opened into a setting room with two lazy boy recliners on one side and a love seat between them. A four foot by four-foot cocktail table, scroll motif, sat modestly in front of the love seat. Directly across from the love seat a sixty-seven inch AVS was mounted on the cabreuva brown wall. There was a desk and chair close to the AVS. The desk had a lamp on it and writing paraphernalia. A computer was sitting on the desk, too. Wall lights accented the AVS on both sides

The floors were Cedro Rosa hard wood with an eighteen foot by twenty-four foot hemp honeycomb area rug gracing the hard wood. A pole lamp stood near the end of the love seat. Straight ahead was the bedroom area. On entering the bedroom a feeling of rest was sensed; it suggested serenity and quiet. A six drawer dressing table, painted celery color with a large mirror 4" x 5" was on the wall directly across from the Queen Sized Bed, a two drawer night stand was on each side of the bed. A phone was on the nightstand to the right of the bed. It was lavish. The kitchen was complete with stove, sink, refrigerator, and microwave oven, as well as an oven for baking or broiling. Bone China was in the cabinets, silverware was in the drawers, an abundance of pots and pans were available, and detergent for washing dishes was in the cabinet. Off to the right of the kitchen was the bathroom complete with shower, bathtub, washbasin, commode, Jacuzzi, and a washer dryer. There was a mirrored medicine cabinet with triple lights over it. The tub had a light over it and a hand held shower control. It was finished in pearl white 4" x 4" porcelain wall and floor tiles. Next to the bathroom was a walk in closet. The Suite had central heat and air. Generic Art works that were bright in color and mood hung casually on the walls. Standing in the entranceway one could see the ocean through the 8" x 6" glass balcony doors.

Many travelers preferred to live with Brazilians during their trips to Brazil. It was a better way to experience the Culture.

The view of the Atlantic Ocean and the white sands of the beach appeared to open their arms embracing them as they stood on the balcony. It was so peaceful and refreshing. There were canvas-backed chairs on the balcony. Totally engulfed in the setting, they sat and took it all in.

It was difficult to get to sleep the first night. Their anticipations of the rest of their stay kept them asking each other, "Are you asleep." Eventually the sun made its yawning entrance in the early Eastern Sky and they leapt from the bed with the spryness and enthusiasm of eight-year-old children.

After breakfast they joined a bicycle tour with the hotel guide. It was very informative. They visited several Historic Sites and the guide told them stories of how and why the sites derived their importance. They toured souvenir shops and bric-a-brac shops as well. They were with a large group of people, forty or so. Everyone got an idea of the locations of the shops and could return at their leisure to buy things. The tour ended at Noon and they returned to their room to eat lunch. They had both worked up an appetite ridding the bikes. After lunch they took a nap. Their not sleeping the night before caught up with them. They awoke at 2:30 p.m. and went for a swim in the hotel pool. After tasting Brahma Beer they both agreed there was no other alcoholic drink with the splendor of it. They had two Brahma lagers each. After that they laid out plans for the rest of the week and it was time for dinner.

Instead of eating in the hotel they decided to see what the nearby restaurants had to offer. Casually strolling north on the street they saw eight Five star eating-places. Of the eight restaurants the El Gaucho was most attractive and enticed. It had a welcoming atmosphere.

At dinner they had a bottle of Two Oceans Merlot and Churrasco with mashed sweet potatoes garnished in a cinnamon butter sauce, and blanched green beans, sautéed in olive oil topped with a garlic dill sauce, for the main meal. It was delicious and left no room for desert. After dinner they meandered the streets of Rio Grande do Sol taking in all the eye could see. It was so colorful, so refreshing and so alive, ending the evening grew more difficult every step they made.

Time melted into memories and three o'clock in the morning came too early, for them. They returned to the Hotel with the excitement weaning and fatigue building. A bed never felt so inviting. Two hours later Sheila felt hot. She had a fever. They got dressed and went to the Hospital. She had contracted a viral infection and needed to be evaluated. In their excitement they completely forgot to put bug spray on. The Doctor advised a bland diet for seven days and as little strenuous activity as possible, considering she was vacationing. He reminded them that the evenings in Brazil are beautiful, but it behooves people to remember the warm night air brings out many mosquitoes. They bite and infect. There were no charges for the visit to the Hospital. Medical care was free everywhere on the planet. Each Nation had determined medical care was a human entitlement. The next day they stayed in the hotel all day.

The following morning they mused over their itinerary. They laughed as most of the itinerary consisted of vigorous activities. A change of plans brought on by Sheila's sudden illness, meant they had to leave the tour for a while. Biking was on tap for the day. The only thing open to them for the day was the Art Museum of Rio Grande do Sul, "Museu de Arte do Rio Grande do Sul, ADo Malagoli." It housed over 1,200 works of art. Institutions in Brazil donated most of the pieces. In the beginning all of the art was bought. Later, after the museum had been established, funds for buying art were withdrawn. The Museum became famous. It was definitely an attraction for tourist. Taking in all the Art the Museum had would easily consume two weeks. They spent four days at the museum.

Most vacationers rode to the Museum on bicycles. There was a large area designated as bicycle parking. No locks or chains were necessary for securing bikes. Brazil was among the first countries to adopt a zero crime tolerance. Prior to the change from a Judicial System that followed the traditional system of the United States and many other Nations, crime was high in Brazil. They had found it increasingly necessary to build more prisons. The cost of maintaining these prisons and the inmates, and the total Judicial System was bankrupting the Country. Plus, the citizenry who was paying the cost for the operation of these institutions was not getting a justifiable return for their continued support. In short, the Judicial System was ineffective. A careful study was conducted and the system was declared out dated and ineffective. The method appealed to the immaturity of those who were empowered to run the Culture in the worst way possible. Their lack of maturity made it a haven for crime, similar to that of the United States.

Growing is difficult. In Brazil as in the United states the majority of the populations had stopped growing at the onset of adulthood. In sane and advanced cultures growth continues after the onset of adulthood and refines itself in maturity. A defining characteristic of maturity is efficient problem solving.

In Progression of Western Civilization by the founders, it had to be crippled for it to need crutches to get around. A setting such as that was suitable for immaturity to flourish. Maturity was suppressed and irresponsibility was encouraged. The punishments for crimes amounted to slaps on the wrists. It was a marriage of nourishing compatibility. The penalties for committing crimes did not either deter or discourage crime. Since the consequences for committing crimes were minimal crime had a field day. That situation existed due to the immaturity of the populace. It was a stagnate culture; there was no growing. Due to the malignant programming the adults had been made to accept as good, they found it sane for people to be at risk from one another.

They had been brainwashed into condescending to acceptance of false ideas of harsh penalties for committing crimes as inhumane human treatments. In 2382 AD, it was proposed and adopted revisions of the consequences for committing crimes must be powerful enough to make a person ponder doing the unacceptable. There were proponents who stood against the revisions in the penal codes. The lobbyists for the status quo were deeply entrenched and finally lost the battle to support the behavior of losers and miscreants. In a reasonably short time, ten years, the people had their say.

As a result, it was mandated the Universal Rules relating to punishments for crimes were adopted by Brazil, 21 May 2394 AD and found appropriate for future criminals to be hospitalized for two days upon conviction. During that two-day stay, surgery, or other measures would be performed to make certain the person would ever after be incapable of committing that crime again. Effective thirty days later, 20 June 2394 there would be zero growth in prison populations and all prisons would be closed six months later.

The old Judicial System was a testament to the insanity level of the citizens, at that time. They were paying taxes to fund a system that was nonproductive. Frankly speaking, the citizens would've been better served by taking their tax money to the window and throwing it in the air. The return on the citizens sustaining the system was an unacceptable return. Crime was on a steady incline instead of a steady decline. There is no way it is possible to validate spending money to correct something and getting more of what is to be corrected as appreciable return on spending as sane behavior. Religious dogma and Forced Miss Education combined as Institutions fit to guarantee the Citizens would remain docile and accept the old Judicial System as the end all.

The old system was bankrupting the Nation. It was highly active, but inactive in productivity. It did not require a college education to view the entire Justice System as an inefficient and ineffective problem-solving agency. Sums of money were flowing into it that ate away at the core of the Nation and added enormous ill appropriated allocations of money into a bottomless pit that in no way was healthy for the National Debt. Considering the populace who administered to the system were learned people from, Harvard, Yale, Princeton, Dartmouth, the Military Academy, the Naval Academy, and the Ivy League camaraderie their problem solving skills proved deficient. The dependence on that group for effective problem solving revealed them as a thicket of bunglers.

Their interests were primarily self-preservation. They stood as a testimonial to the damage Forced Miss education posses in human development. Citizens funded the Government and the Warlocks received the benefits. Eventually 'Truth' triumphed and the house of lies came tumbling down. Change is always a threat to the status Quo. Nevertheless, it is necessary. It was done.

There was a domino effect. Since no more criminals were being locked up, crime dwindled. The change was totally efficient, and the prison system was dismantled. It took forty years in the United States. The corruption ran deep.

Finally the Citizens were getting what they were entitled to for funding a Justice System, Justice, Respect and Safety. It took over seventy years in total to accomplish the change. Brazil was one of the first Countries to adopt a zero crime tolerance. The United States was the very last Nation to implement it. It embraced the practice in 2515 AD. The battle for change started in 2475 AD in the United States and it was resolved in favor of the people on 19 June 2515 AD The corruption ran so deep in the United States that it took that long to vacuum it up. It was like unto an eleven-month-old male brat kicking and screaming in a tantrum with his mentally retarded parents looking on.

It was late when they decided to call it a day. Their Hotel was close to the Museum, which was located in the center of town. As they walked to the Hotel from the bike rental shop people greeted them and smiled. Vibrant gaiety of colors surround them and fed their souls: the shops with their dazzling displays in the show windows, the people clothed in bright uplifting colors, women with garland of wild flowers around their necks. Garlands with creativity that demanded their heads swivel from side to side to catch glimpses of each one, as the people passed by. Many of the women wore wild flower in their hair. The rich deep-blackness of their hair made a mesmerizing background for black, white, and orange wildflower groupings. Not to be out done "Flor Do CerrADo" a yellow flower was a firm competitor. It had the distinction of the best of festive aplomb for many years. It was easy to submit to the sensual beckoning of Hibiscus Rosa Sinensis resting on the wavy dark rich black hair of the women. The air was filled with a fragrance of tranquility and well-being. It felt soothing on their faces. All around people wore festive hats and bright colored outfits. Still others adorned their hair with garlands of wildflowers, intricately woven into hair arrangements and styles. It was a breath giving mosaic of happy people sculpted on a tropical canvas.

The changes in the System brought about improvements in sociability. People could trust one another. There was no need to lie, cheat, steal, or exploit. Education focused on social development

Cooperative living was necessary on the part of all humans, and using each other to practice perfection by maintaining brotherly and sisterly appreciation for each other. Bamboozling each other was no longer practiced, respected, nor tolerated.

This restructuring of the function of formal education was dissociative to jobs and more in association with meaningful work. People worked at what they enjoyed with the intention of making a positive contribution to their communities. They avoided all things that were contrary to the welfare of the environment. The revamped education allowed them to view themselves as a part of everything. Damaging any part of the whole was the same as damaging themselves. Acquiring that knowledge allowed them to see the wisdom in preservation of the environment. Theirs was the task of consciously maintaining balance of all natural life. The old systems instructed modify natural life to meet their wants and wishes. Its attitude was 'Who cares about the environment's balance or disrupting it.' The elders understood real things in life work to maintain balance instinctively. Man was the only creature who was given the discretion to maintain the environment or destroy it. Mankind had tricked Man into destroying it. Now the time had come for the people to wake up. More people were believing in God and their forms of worship too were changed. Religion became a discipline, a way of life.

Religion too had had its inoculations against stagnation. Islam was no different; it had grown. The new generation of Muslims no longer sought the aggressive and negative ways of the West.

The long-standing greeting to one another among Muslims is, "Peace be with you." Before 2099 AD Muslims did not live in that fashion. Muslims did not act peaceful. Most Muslims thought it logical to vent violence upon others to bring about Peace. It took a great deal of maturity for them to realize Peace is not to be found in Violence. Anger and Ire are the twins born of Violence. Others were known to beat and mistreat their wives. Truly the lives lived by Muslims of that era were no way reflective of projecting Peace. Their words and their behavior contradicted each other. It was a big topic of discussion throughout the Islamic World. Finally, an Imam asked an Amir, "Do you believe violence has the potential to bring about World Peace?" Neither the Amir nor anyone else would attempt to answer the question, in Truth. Instead they began to diligently work to harness violence and tame it.

Upon hearing of the dilemma, Imam abbas bin abdl saleem sent a plea to all Islamic Orders of to convene and formulate a clear and concise understanding of how best to live God's declaration of, "Either the true believers will be victorious or they will go straight to Paradise."

The Summit Meeting was held 12 February 2096 AD at Lagos, Nigeria. The findings of the Summit Attendees were to be delivered to Council of Elders. The Elders were to formally address the conclusion of the Islamic Summit. After fifteen months of being deadlocked on what the Quran meant by "victory or Paradise for the believers" a venerable Muslim Cleric was consulted.

Umdat al Mumeen said," Believers must one day die. That is an event in the hands of Almighty Allah. When one Man may raises his hand to kill another Man, he is choosing to defy the Will of Allah. It is a known that God has commanded us in this fashion, 'Thou shall not kill.' It is against God's will for any man to kill another Man." He continued, "Violence in Islam was the baby of Islam. The baby has become a fully mature adult and has become whole.

This wholeness demands Muslims understand the JihAD is no longer conquering others, it is conquering self. That is a most difficult war to wage. In it one must master-self and bow to the will of Allah. There is nothing more meaningful for the believers than submitting to the Will of Allah. "Thou shall not kill," means exactly that, "No killing." There are no exceptions to Allah's decree.

There is a fountain of rewards for those who keep themselves well under control and do as Allah has instructed. Allah has treasures unmeasured for those who read his word and follow. These gifts are available through self-mastery. God has it arranged that non-believers have two choices. The first choice is leave the believers alone. That is a victory for the believers. The other choice is for the non-believer is to kill the believer. When the non-believer makes this choice he sends the dying believer directly to Paradise. Muslims have no call to fighting and violence anymore. We have a guarantee of either work to bring about God's will on Earth or dwell in Paradise." It is a win, win for the true believer. Hence forth we must be the example of Peace unto all the world."

In answer to the question, "Violence knows not the way to Peace. Violence is the road to power and control of others. No where is it to be found that power ever leads to peace No matter what the challenge, we must keep ourselves under our control and not the control of others. In so doing we affirm our faith and our trust in Allah, God. As devout Muslims we are the only chance the World has of salvation. Violence serves the purpose of the infidels and non-believers. The mentally weak and physically feeble are stricken with fear of death or pain. The physically, strong and spiritually strait have overcome the fears of either death, or pain."

May 29, 2100 AD it was resolved violence would no longer be welcome in Islam. Muslims all over the World embraced the transition of Islam and adopted a more wholesome regard for Allah. They were the example of finest servants of God. The resolution was adopted by the United States in 2496 AD.

By the year 2501 every Religion had abandoned preaching 'Hell fire and brimstone.' Firstly, Religious instruction was now declaring there are nothing but beginnings on this Journey through life. Religion had featured fear, reprisals and the threat of Death to burden the progeny of every faith. Secondly, the probability of no ending gave the people a spirit of Liberation that defied oppression, subjugation, and or colonization. Religion was an instrument of possibilities. The change made them eager candidates for the meeting with their Maker.

Those two changes removed the burdensome mantles of despair from the people shoulders, world wide, and replaced it with spiritual garments of mirth. Indeed Religion had evolved to instruct the ways of Truth and Joyous rejoicing in God. The entire vibration of the universe had moved to higher vibration frequencies. The love for God and one an-other filled the cells of all things in all places, bar none.

God was no longer seen as a "Big Bully" anxiously waiting for men and women to error or sin, so He could punish them. No, the new understanding of HIM and them presented HIM as a loving, caring parent who was ever steadfast in HIS guidance and mercy. A parent who readily extends a guiding hand to those who were willing to return to HIM, a parent who was filled with love for all of HIS children. A parent who was ever ready to welcome back to HIS guidance any of HIS children who strayed.

The elevator stopped at their floor and they stepped out. Neither of them said a word. Instead, they dashed into the suite, and they lay on the bed enfolded in each other's arms and drifted into the dream of sleep. From that point on the pace was quickened and the days ran into each other drenching them in happiness. Before they knew it they were on an airplane heading home.

The total Brazil experience was a thing to remember. There was a moment when it transformed them and they knew life would ever after be new. It was during the time when Sheila was injured. They had gone for a bike ride. It was a dirt road at the edge of the city. Soothing fragrances filled the air and birds sang joyously to serenade the day. They had been riding for about an hour when they came upon a gathering of people on the side of a hill. They stopped. The people were there to listen to the words of an Elder Shaman. He was talking about Love.

It was a gathering of over two hundred people. The Shaman was standing on a slight knoll fifty feet in front of the closest people.

He spoke almost in a whisper. Yet, his voice was as audible and clear to the outer edges of the group. His words come up from the deeper recesses of the people's souls and were heard inside of them. They had never before experienced hearing with the inner ear of spirit.

He said, "True Love is a bonding over time. Lust is a false emotion of the moment. Before there can ever be love there must be friendship. Friendship takes time to develop and is the main part of loving. Friends know neither treachery nor deceit as trustworthy acquaintances in developing deep, rich, and true love. Friends have divorced themselves from selfishness. Friends seek to be irreplaceable compliments to the lives of the ones they love. A true friend will do all he or she can to avoid bringing hurt or disappointment to their friend."

"Love will not come to partner with any others than friends. Love takes up residency where friendship is lord of the land. People who are established in friendship take care of one another. This caring for one another builds a bond of trust. It is this trust that assures the heart it is safe to open and give of itself unendingly. Any other paring is a fraudulent embarrassment to love."

He continued, "Many have learned and believe loving is controlling another. Truly loving someone is allowing them space to be who they must be, all the while continuing to love them. In their ignorance many mistake lust for love. A woeful fact of this mistake is children that are born of lust, as opposed to love, usually are unwanted. The people they enter the world through have neither time nor loving concern for them. Subsequently many are abused, molested, and neglected."

"In loving relationships mature adults have foresight enough to enter the sexual act with the intentions of bringing someone into life they can show love to. The two love one another and may feel bringing a person into the world will bless their existence by expanding their love for one another into and through a child. Loving parents practice loving their children."

"Lust's child is a problem and an inconvenience to immature adults. These adults enter sexual acts for sensual gratification. They are not interested in loving a child or the parenting of a child. Lust has them in its clutches and they are void of love for one another. They are in it for the fun."

He could not get angry about that condition. There are so many tragedies tied into this than are apparent. Of them the greatest tragedy is, they believe they are awake and competent. Believe it or not, lust finds accommodations in the sleepers among Man. This is truth. Whether, or not one believes truth to be truth, is of no consequence to Truth. Truth will be truth.

"The shaman continued, "Relationships held together with lust are usually rocky and violent. The driving force in lust relationships is control. Generally relationships in which one mate claims the other as "theirs" are dark relationships. Lust is a smothering thing. It restricts and allies itself with fear and insecurity. It drives men to beat women and to be jealous. It even drives some men into killing women."

"The companion of lust is pleasure. Lust is pleasure driven and extremely dangerous. The reason it is dangerous is; it is fickle. Lust is ever in search of new pleasures. It has no requirement or necessity for a relationship. It is always in a flux and fickle. It is loyal to itself, only. Lust is bonded by sensual pleasure. That bond will ever prove faulty and flawed."

"Many humans believe, sex is an important part of loving someone. Sex has nothing to do with love. The main function of sex is procreation. When sex and lust combine and are the total substance of a relationship, no substantial relationship exists. People do not have to be in love to have sex with each other. The force that brings a prostitute and a client together is lust. Thus, the time they spend together will be very short and very abrupt." The people caught in these webs of deception misapply the word love for the acts. To shelter themselves from facing themselves they call it love. It isn't. All the while they are swirling in lust. They know not the difference between the two. Males and females prowl the earth searching for the look of lust in others eyes. The look of lust is what many search for and call it the look of love. They mistakenly identify it as love. This happens when two people look upon opposites as sexually objects, instead of beings to partner with on the journey through life."

He continued, "In the animal world they have sex. They do it to procreate. There is no love involved in animal or insect sex acts. Birds do it. Bees do it and love has nothing to do with it. It is a gross mistake to believe sex is a prime factor for love."

The shaman ended his talk and turned toward a mountain in the far distance. Each step he took appeared to shed a tear for the many sadness caused by lust. There was stillness and quiet among the ones gathered to hear him share his understanding of love. The eyes of all were focused on his departure. As he grew more distant from the gathering his physical body became less visible and his inner glow became an external energetic light. It was evident there were no dark forces, in any amount, capable of dimming the spiritual light he had become to the World. Were a King Cobra to bite him, the venom would instantly become lemonade. Soon there was no visible trace of his physical body. There was a brilliantly bright cipher of light that was in reality him. It began to rise higher and higher as he ascended into the Heavens. He passed the seven Heavens; his destination was the Kingdom of God.

Although experiences such as that were common among the Brazilians, it was brand new for visitors such as He and Sheila, too. Neither of them had ever experienced the presence of beings not of this Earth. That part of the trip changed them both into better versions of themselves, and they knew without question the change was permanent.

He became aware of His being blind, deaf, and dumb until that passage of time. The things He had heard, seen, and understood found fertile ground to seed in and He saw Himself differently. He had truly gone away and found Himself. Sheila had been quiet all the while He was involved in His reverie said to Him, "It was a great vacation. One I will cherish for the rest of my time on Earth." He tilted His head to the right and smiled accordingly

Chapter

14

SANITY OR INSANITY

SEATED ON THE AIRPLANE He asked himself, how can I know I am sane? What is the measure for sanity? Who sets the standard for sanity? Theses questions invaded His mind as He traversed the skyways of His mind. Silently He wrestled with these questions most of the flight.

The next day began with Him still puzzled about the bedrock of sanity and why it was so unclear to Him. For the first time in His life He was aware that there was a line of departure between is and isn't. The line was thin and subtle. For that reason it could be manipulated and tampered with by mankind. He became cognizant of the struggle between mankind, or Satan and Man, a condition brought on by waking up. As long as a Man was a sleepwalker mankind paid him little attention. When Man woke up the struggle began. Sanity will always be actions that reflect cause and Insanity will always be actions that reflect effect. The sane man is cause. The insane kind of man is effect. Sanity is the self. Insanity is the not self.

Therefore, Sanity must be determined as positive actions intended to perfect one's own existence or being. Then, sanity is behavior that appreciates and understands harmony and balance. Insanity does just the opposite. The more one perfects their being all the more they become positive as opposed to negative in the spiritual sense. The more positive one is, the saner one is. It is this saneness that promotes ascension into the origin of all that is, all that has been, and all that will ever be in the future. Saneness is a matrix that in its higher planes of constancy is neither male, nor female. It simply is. That part of becoming self may be very confusing for some. It helps to study nature for clarity at times. Nature follows the Will of God and is never led astray. Satan follows his own will and is destined to find being misled the direction he is traveling in.

Saneness is the constant establishing oneself into being, which starts self-extinction. When self-extinction is realized non-being is the state of ones condition. Non-being is sanity in its near absolute form. When non-being merges into Peace saneness is in its infancy. In this state of non-being, one is lost in the One and all other states and conditions no longer impinge upon self. The realization attained here is that the One is 'the Nothing' and it transcends all states of even the Grandest, Existence because the nothing is everything. The "Nothing" is the origin of all that is. As such it is the returning point for all that is. Here there is neither contingency, nor condition. Sanity is beginning and reality is no longer a quandary.

Simple adherence to "Do unto others as you would have them do unto you," ends the quandary and true being or existence begins. The dilemma about what is right and what is wrong no longer weighs upon the shoulders of Man. It is resolved. Man is ever after liberated and has achieved the highest success life is capable of offering. What follows this beginning is sanity, Self. The trial dimension of existence no longer exists and the traveler is released from returning or reincarnating, involuntarily. Self has been found.

The quandary is wrapped up in a nice little package of knowing right from wrong, and real from unreal. Sanity then, may be found in behavior that holds peace of mind. When sanity determines actions self is in control. Through the attainment of self-annihilation love is the only condition that affects self. That love is love of God and love for all that is God's. What is to be done is known and exceeds the expectations of form, function, or rewards. None have reason to question the why of a person's actions, because it is self-vindicating and reason, logic, and purpose all stand open and clearly revealed in the individual's actions.

This level of sanity is an ideal state of consciousness to realize self. There are others. Here who a person is goes beyond the temporary physical self. The true self is the operator of the temporary physical self. It is not temporary. The true or real self has no beginning neither does it have an ending. It is the origin of "Nothing".

At the end of the idea of beginning and ending, the sane reach the Alter of union with the Creator. Them, Self-annihilation become that self which is in everything. When it is complete one has achieved self-annihilation. Better stated, the personal self ceases to be one's focus. The focus is on the impersonal self, the ONE. Here the truly sane person no longer exists separate and a part from all that is and non-being is realized as transition to Bliss. It is the immersion into all as a part of one whole that unites the domains that lie beyond existence, immortality, and eternity.

Conversely, insanity is characterized by behavior that promotes indolence and destructive aggressive preoccupation with destroying or corrupting completely healthy culture's behaviors, traditions, mores, etc. The insane have no sense of self, so their objective is to control others. A consistent characteristic of people who lack self-control is they justify why they should be in control of others lives. That is characteristic of Satanism, which is the way of Imperialism, Capitalism, Democracy, and Monarchy as well. Everything they do is designed to take what others are using, and control others reality. They advance a doctrine of freedom, for all. Freedom is exactly what they wind up taking. They hide their true purpose, enslaving and making everyone insane. In essence the insane, replace reality with either a False Reality or a Forced Reality.

Both False Reality and Forced Reality are Forms of Function. They modify, combine, and Universal Principles and Laws that are appealing to Man's lower nature and trap him into enslavement, i.e. mechanical gadgets, etc.

Capitalism, Imperialism, and Democracy deny people freedom. They all interwoven into one thing, 'sophisticated slavery.' The only people, who have opportunities to reach freedom, in the above social systems, are the stingy, sociopathic, greedy or the cunning. People who are caring, equitable, and pious are regarded as fuel to satisfy the demands of the scruples appetites of those who have no self-control, and no scruples what so ever, the insane.

The more peace one has in their life; the saner they are. This sanity and peace partnership holds true for individuals, organizations, groups, Countries, and The World as well. Sanity at all levels is host to Peace. Insanity is always the bedfellow of war, hostility, aggression, and confusion. Denial generally follows acts of insanity.

It is known some leaders have purposely committed violent acts upon their people to insight the people to war against an unsuspecting group. Those leaders will deny any wrong doing until the day they die. They are insane and have no regard for Truth.

He was thankful for not being caught up in negative spiral of actions for which He would not claim ownership. Denial of ones inappropriate actions is insane. He could see at a glance the acts that required a person to hide behind lies and deceit demonstrated clearly insane behavior. The fact that the act is outrageously insane is openly apparent, because the person performing the act denies ownership of it.

A person is what he or she does more so than what a person thinks, eats, or lays claims to being. An alleged felon who submits a plea of not guilty related to the commission of a crime that the felon knows was committed by him, is insane. However, this denial does not exempt the person from being held accountable for the commission of the act. By entering a not guilty plea he has announced his insanity, only. He knows he did it, but he is saying he did not do it. He wants to get away with it. Some attorneys are advocates for this type of insanity. They advise clients to enter pleas of not guilty to things done by them. These types of attorneys are not concerned about Truth. They enjoy word games, which proves they are insane.

It is as basic as an adult exceeding the speed limit and getting a ticket. For the adult to deny speeding is insanity. Their denial of ownership of exceeding the speed limit serves as a declaration of their insanity. This adult has no sense of self and no awareness of self-mastery, at all. Unless adults mature they will go through life perfecting their insanity, only.

Came a time when a massive return to sanity occurred among the down trodden. It was during the reconstruction period. The Country had gone through another recession and people were losing their homes at record pace. The banks were foreclosing mercilessly and dispossessing families as if they were in competition with one another to see who could evict the most families per day. The pressure on the families was beyond description. One man lost it. When the sheriff knocked on his door with an eviction notice he did something that would change the method of providing shelter for families forever, in the land.

Very politely this man extended his hand for the sheriff's agent to place the notice to vacate in his hand. Upon receiving the notice the man stepped back into the home he had made payments on for twenty-two years and picked up a chair, which he placed in the middle of the street. Item by item was taken from his home, by him, and placed in the middle of the street. Soon there was no way for automobile traffic to use the street. His personal belongings had completely sealed off the street. His neighbors saw what he was doing. When he had satisfied the notice to vacate, he poured gasoline on all of his belongings and lit a match to them.

There were thirty-seven homes on that street. Nineteen of the homes were under notice to vacate, by order of the bank. His neighbors quickly began to follow his example. It finally dawned on the rest of his neighbors what was happening to the nineteen families could eventually happen to them. It was time to stop this from ever happening again. The system for providing shelter for the people was not broken, neither was it defective. If anything it was diabolical. Ironically enough deficiencies were built into it. It simply did not work. As it stood it would ever return to the status quo. Future generations would find themselves in the same predicament. Any attempt at retaining the same system of providing shelter for people, without a doubt, was an obvious case of ineptitude in problem solving. It was not people friendly. It had never worked because; it was false. It was a False Reality.

Realizing this to be factual families being evicted moved all of their things from their homes into the street and burned them. Within a week the entire city was gridlocked, as everybody who was under eviction notice from the banks, did the same thing. Over night the practice swept through the nation. Government at all levels was baffled. What could they do to end this civil disobedience; it was their dilemma. The proper choice was the least desirable for the Banking Industry and Governments as well. They met and met. Many discussions were by telephone as the Cities were all gridlocked. Not one single thing was operating. The obstruction of the streets had caused schools to close, hospitals to close, fire stations to close, police stations to close, stores to close, restaurants to close, and cessation of all deliveries or repairs. It resolved when the evictions stopped and those who suffered due to the practice received full restitution.

As always in the struggle that is inherent in the battle between good and evil, innocent people die. It matters little whether the death comes through violence or disobedience it happens. Death must never stand as a reason to suffer under oppression. Those who die for Truth have truly lived most. They have walked with their hands in God's hand. They were sane.

Evil had no recourse other than accept the effect of its flagitious deception, because it was a lie. All who died during the transformation from the old system of providing housing would have all their sins cast upon the people who supported the old system. Any descent things the wicked had accrued in life would be awarded to the innocents who died, as a result of the wickedness, in the next dimension. Likewise all sins or transgressions of the innocents were transferred to the devilish who support the evils of fraud and deception.

Such is the just fortune of insanity. Innocence is a willing host for sanity. Sanity is the guardian of Peace and Peace is the Goal.

There is a clear distinction between the two and in His resolve He had clearly set them apart the one from the other. Insanity seeks safety, certainty, or security. Those things are unavailable in this temporary journey. The insane surround themselves with insecurity. They acquire stuff that requires protection and insurance against loss. Everything the insane owns is insured by a company that is betting the things will not be stolen, lost or damaged. The only thing the insane buy that does not require insurance against loss or damage is Time Sharing. That people cold be persuaded to buy time is the most glaring example of insane behavior. A person has to be thoroughly insane to buy time to use an object conjointly with twenty-six other couples. It is supposed to guarantee a place for vacationing two weeks, once a year. It's insane. In essence the couples buy time, not the structure. Being insane it makes perfect sense to engage in such acts. The insane are so accustomed to wanting they will buy time. It was not at all surprising when they started selling areas of outer space.

There was a period when they bought Pet Rocks. The rocks were common sand stone readily found in abundance on many beaches. Some entrepreneur hit upon the idea of putting these rocks in cute little boxes with straw in them and selling them for as much as one hundred and seventy-five dollars. Well-formally educated middle-class people would buy a birth certificate for fifteen dollars, with the rock. They were known to take their Pet Rocks for rides in their cars and walks in the park. They threw parties and celebrated their rocks birthdays. Guests were known to bring birthday presents to parties for rocks. This was a rampant practice among the middle class of people in the United States of America. That behavior was inappropriate and most certainly bazaar in rationale, and insane by any standard of human mental, or spiritual development.

During that period of extreme insanity pet rock owners engaged in taking their pet rocks everywhere they went. Some hAD parties expressly for their pet rocks. Others took their pet rocks to the beach and put them on small blankets so the rocks could get a tan. They took them on trips to parks so they could meet other per rocks. When they vacationed they took them with them or had someone look in on their pet rock while they were away. Think about that, the formally educated paid someone to rock sit.

How was it possible for them to assess a value for a commonly found stone, unless it was a through a state of pre-imposed and preconditioned planned insanity.

On the other hand, the sane seek no such treasures as safety, certainty, or security. The sane know all states being and non-being are temporary states. Losses and gains are arbitrarily concepts that warrant the maximum amount of indifference. One day all that a person has will be left behind. What one man may determine as a loss is open to determination of another man as gain. In truth no item has a value. A sane person knows the accorded and agreed upon value of an item is merely attributable to the ridiculousness' of Satan. The sane don't want. The sane don't waste. The sane mature adult knows there are no guarantees in life of anything lasting. The sane man gives thanks for his daily bread. The insane man wants a guarantee that there will be bread tomorrow.

He understood sanity and insanity for the first time.

Chapter

15

IRON BARS DO NOT A JAIL MAKE

LIBERATION IS THE HIGHEST success this experience holds. It is the treasure of treasures. Liberation is the result of self-mastery. When one masters-self Liberation is the result. Liberation is a level of being beyond Total Bliss. It is the Path that empties of its bounty into Self. Then the One is the path and the Path is the One. All separate vanishes and the One only is left. Ever reviving and energizing it vibrates on and on. In discovering self the optimum reward is attained. It is the only thing that can be taken from this temporal experience. It is consciousness at the level of release to the bondage of returning to Earth, involuntarily.

Freedom differs from Liberation. Freedom lives and dies in external conditions, outward circumstances, and dependencies. It differs most from Liberation in that it can be given by another or withdrawn by another. Freedom is not the Goal. It is a lure. It is an imaginary concoction that entraps the consciousness and stymies self-mastery.

The confusion is easily settled when we see the two for their content. Freedom has no content. The word suggests something is being withheld. It is powerful enough to persuade people into feeling external conditions in their lives lack some meaningful substance. The mental state that accompanies that feeling is a form of Jail.

Realizing that fact reveals someone has control over things. Whatever the thing is has value, because it is being withheld. Once the barrier is removed and access is permitted the game is over. That starts another game. The main parts of the games are contingencies or conditions. i.e. Young people, eighteen to twenty-one may feel freedom is theirs, because their parents allow them to stay out until 11:00 p.m. The City Officials may implement a curfew requiring all young people, specifically eighteen to twenty-one, must be home by 10:00 p.m. Other people might be convinced they are free because, they can be spontaneous, and irresponsible. Yet another group may be convinced they have freedom because, they do whatever pleases them. It suggests the extending of unlimited rights of exclusion to individuals, groups, or organizations to do as he, she, or it pleases.

Such was the case in North America during slavery. Under the auspices support and favor of England slavery was looked upon with approval. The Colonizers or Slave Masters made up a fictitious rule that declared Africans were three fifths of a human. Where did the authority to make that declaration come from? They had no authority other than Witch Craft and Violent Nature to support the declaration. It was spurred on by the pursuit of self-indulgence, self-aggrandizement, and privilege. In examining the idea of do as you please, it becomes apparent freedom is not only a false idea, but also an unsustainable idea. It causes more problems than it resolves.

Over doing anything will consistently result in some problem resulting in the need to apply temperance. No matter whether it is eating too much, drinking too much, or whatever too much the result will invariably prove to be unfavorable. For the most part Freedom has connoted irresponsibility and unaccountability. People who sought Freedom associated being out of control as being free. These are empty promises of something from something that has no substantive part of self in its make up. Things that have no substance in them are lacking in content and are the equivalent to stagnation. Freedom is a hoax.

Existence precedes all else. However, that Truth does not deserve the cavalier approach of those who in their flight to freedom violate natural function. In the end choices determine final destinations. Subsequently, Existence cannot be compromised by aberrant behaviors such as homosexuality. No matter how widespread it may become, same sex acts defy natural function and cannot be covered under the canon of existence.

It would be grand, for some, were freedom to lead to Liberation. Such is not the case. That unrestrained mode of life is license to facilitate imbalance in the natural order. The mass production of automobiles proved harmful to the environment and disrupted the ecological balance.

In the past one man's freedom has resulted in hardships and various forms of slavery for others. People who had no self-control heralded Freedom. They used it to deny autonomy to the innocent people. History reports they pillaged, plundered, and took what others had and became rulers in the others land. People who have self-control live and let live.

History, also reports the Africans were minding their own affairs and life was good. Then, it happened out of control barbarians invaded their land and disrupted the structure of their culture. Anthropologic studies support the reality of African Cultures being highly developed, by African Standards, before 1600. The first thing the barbarians and invaders set about was destroying the families, next was the exchange system, and last was the Religion.

The most fallacious act was alleging the barbarians were civilized and the Africans were Savages. The reverse was True. The barbarians put the Continent of Africa in Jail. First, he cooperated with the barbarians. That proved to be a mistake. So he fought the barbarians. That proved to be disastrous. Violence is the barbarians' nature.

The African was defending his Culture, family, and his way of life. The barbarians attributed characteristics peculiar to his nature to that of the African. It was the invaders who were Savages. It is documented some Africans were able to exit their bodies at will. That is most certainly a characteristic of an extremely developed Culture in being.

The word civilized does not hold sociability as its primary value. On the contrary, it suggests rues, eating with a knife and fork, using a napkin and other superficial behaviors. Nowhere in history did it acknowledge the African was spiritually eons ahead of the barbarians. They couldn't. To do so, they would be submitting a disclaimer for the justifications they offered explaining their atrocious acts. The barbarians' insanity drove them to convince themselves what they were doing was right. What it did was put the spiritual evolution of man back five hundred thousand years, minimum. The human experience would've benefited more had the barbarians studied with the Africans instead of putting them in chains and selling them as property. In the barbarians' quest for freedom, they Jailed themselves and the African.

Privilege is an errant aspect of freedom, which is, itself a false condition. Freedom works best when small groups thrive and the larger groups suffer or struggle. At best the idea of Freedom makes it acceptable for the selfish, the greedy, and the immature adults to avoid sharing the commonwealth of life, equally. The claim of Democracy is, "It is a system that allows equal opportunity for all." In a Democracy the people who rise to the top are the greedy, low down, socially deficient ones. They exploit and misuse everything and everybody on their way to excess. The civilized did a lot of dirt in the name of Democracy.

Conclude Freedom means you have actualized, and you will have arrived at a wrong conclusion. Further, that you are at liberty to have special concessions and privileges over others, wrong again. These conclusions indicate you have chosen the wrong direction on the Path, due to your immaturity. Although there is but one Path, there are two directions to choose. One directional choice leads to higher self and the ultimate success this journey has as a reward, for a life well lived. The other directional choices lead away from self and the ultimate failure this journey has as a reprisal, for a life ill lived.

Freedom implies a lack of self-management and ramped with conditions. It is totally intertwined to the physical world and casually affiliated to the spiritual world. The Freedom seeker leaves this world in a complicated state of self-abnegation. In truth each person is composed of more spiritual energy and presence than physical matter.

The improper direction leads to temporal pleasures, self-indulgences, lusts, wants, improprieties, lies, denial, Freedoms, and Insanity. Each of the above is a form of Jail. It is the lot of the miss-guided. Proper direction leads to peace of mind, peace on Earth, self-restraint, love, needs, propriety, sanity, and Liberation.

Liberation has no contingencies neither does it have physical conditions. Many people do what they believe is best to gain Heaven or at worst, avoid Hell. The Master of self has no such agenda. The master of self knows the more right things done, the more right one becomes. It follows the more right one becomes the saner one is. The saner one is the more self one is. The more self one is the more liberated One is.

Liberation is causal and fixedly an irrevocable state of being. The liberated are constant cause and never effect. Unlike physical acquisitions those reaching the Plane of Liberation are able to leave this world with it as their companion. Liberation is the master finding him or herself. The Liberated soul leaves this world in this state of spiritual being or existing. Liberation is a state of Existence far removed from mere survival.

The Knower of the known aspires to reach the liberated state of being. It is the only thing a person who knows searches for. The knower is One who has awakened. When a person leaves this life all the physical things they acquired, must be left behind. The intangible things they have been awarded or accorded by their piers, must also left behind. Liberation can be taken with people when they exit life. It is a state of attained consciousness. It is the bounty of life experience. It is success at its highest pentacle.

Liberation is energy. It is not something one can buy at the corner store or the major discount store. It is an unseen thing. There are many unseen things e.g. anger, pain, pleasure, and sympathy are all unseen things. Liberation rates higher than major unseen things, because unlike most of them nothing affects it, or causes it. Most unseen things are subject to outside influences, liberation is not. Liberation is a thing, an energy that is permanent.

Best example of a liberated person, which comes to mind, is Mahatma Gandhi. He was neither saint nor sinner: he was a liberated man. He used it to present Truth. The Imperialistic British tried every dirty tactic in the book to break him, so they could continue to subjugate the Hindus in India. He was so liberated that he was ready to suffer, be beaten, locked up, or die but he was not willing to either fight or kill the British invaders. He was ready to give his life for the misconduct of the British. His liberated state would not bring him to compromise with the British.

Some Hindu people died violent deaths at the hands of the British to secure independence from England. The Hindu people followed the example of their Spiritual leader and remained non violent. The non-cooperation policy, with evil, vexed the British to no end. The colonizing Queen of England insisted the Hindus accept the degradation of England as just and fair. Her Majesty with her army was willing to kill unarmed women, elderly, and children to maintain England's hold on the Hindu people. The Hindu movement was too powerful for the clutches of evil, Britain. Eventually the Hindus broke Jail and the British barbarians went back to England.

People who are properly educated attain to Liberation first. The problem with proper education was it is impossible to instill fear in people who are liberated. The old system worked very efficiently, because the people were afraid of everything. They were afraid to live and afraid to pass on. The old system worked best, because it black mailed, bullied, coerced, threatened, intimidated, and punished people. The British oriented the people to reprisals through formal education as acceptable conditions for them. Formal education only prepared people to fit into slots necessary to be filled for the rulers, warlocks, and slave masters to enjoy lavish living. In exchange the people acquired the bottom row in Maslow's Hierarchy of Needs by earning money. The only way to get the money was to do what the slave masters demanded. The old system was not friendly. It was imprisonment of the worst kind.

Vocation is secondary in educating people. Primarily, education had to emphasize Man is first, last, and always cause and effect in his life. What is inherent in Liberation is people learn to neither seek the attainment of Heaven, nor seek the avoidance of Hell. They simply focus on doing the right thing. They become cause for the sustaining of a better World. A final example of a liberated person may be seen in this short story.

A merchant was traveling and vending his wares. A young woman came to him and beseeched him to free her from a man who was holding her against her will. She had run away from her family. A stranger offered her a place to live. She accepted his offer; later on the stranger told her she had to sell her body to repay him. He presented her with an ultimatum sell your body for money and give the money to him, or he would beat her. She was frightened. She was trembling as she told the merchant the story.

The merchant got her address and instructed her to be there and ready to leave the next day at 3:00 p.m. At 3:00 p.m. the merchant arrived. While the merchant was waiting for the young woman to collect her things, (she did not believe the merchant was going to help her), the man came. He looked at the merchant and went in the back of the house, where the young woman had gone. Moments later the young woman returned with her belongings and she and the merchant departed. The merchant took her to a female friend's home. Some time later the young woman wrote the merchant a letter stating she had a job as a waitress and was going to college, to earn a degree.

The merchant was a liberated man. The man who was holding the young woman against her will knew what he was looking at when he looked into the eyes of the merchant. The merchant was prepared to give his life for the young girl. The stranger understood the merchant's position. He no longer was a threat to the young woman. That is the power of Liberation.

Liberation is cordial to those who do right. That sounds difficult. It sounds abstract. It is neither difficult nor abstract. It is too, too simple. Right is doing unto others, as you would have them do unto you. That is why it is so transparent that the throne of England knew slavery was wrong. Neither the King nor the Queen would like to be enslaved by others. The throne of England stands guilty of committing the worst sin of all sins, doing things to others that they know they would not want done to them.

Doing the right thing is never as easy as falling off a rolling log, but it leads to Liberation. It is more than anything tangible can deliver.

It is being at the highest level of energy experiencing life. It is the door to the release from the wheel of birth, death, and reincarnation.

Unlike freedom Liberation is a realm outside of conditions. It is growth into self and unscripted. For it is ever new and ever changing. It is spiritual growth and becoming more of who we are. The non-liberated may attempt to discredit the possibility of attaining Liberation. Let them. Only the true believer will realize Liberation. Faith is ones agent. Likewise, non-liberated may try to create doubt and undermine the understanding acquired by the faithful. Beseech them not. Non-believers may attempt to add conditions and request the believer to perform tricks. Liberation is not that.

As a Liberated person develops the realm of the possible increases. It is a progression similar to any other transition. It begins in the pit of modified ineptitude. As the cells of the body embrace the vibrations of spirit the impossible becomes possible. What remains as impossible is anything or anybody posing a danger of any kind to the liberated soul. Attempting to harm or hinder such a One is fruitless as attempting to dab fragrances beams of light. In the state of Liberation a person is not the body. The person remains in the body as the operator of the body, only. The Liberated person is not this, but that. The things the un-liberated seek have neither meaning, nor significance to the Liberated.

A clump of clay and a nugget of gold are the same to the Liberated. These things are symbolic of duality, which is false reality. To believe a nugget of gold has value in life is insane. Were gold to be left in the bowels of the earth it would have neither a critical, nor a crucial impact on life. No one would starve, or faint, or become ill. Without natures production of Oranges people can become ill. So Oranges have value as being necessary for life to go on. The manipulators assign value to gold. The liberated understand the difference.

The Liberated live lives of spiritual alchemy. Liberated beings take on negative energies and currents and neutralize their expansion and growth. Negative incidents become spiritual Gold to the believers. Negative spirits become fuel for the Liberated Spiritual Alchemist. Liberated beings are born into the world positive and remain that way. Negative spiritual energies often get trapped by Liberated Spiritual Beings. Liberated beings are positive spirit and cannot be altered. Negative energy is used as balance for them. It keeps them from becoming too heady. It can be identified by certain consistent characteristics known to the knower. The primary characteristic Negative is it always takes, swindles, and connives. When negative gives it is preparing to take several times more than it gave in return.

The Liberated turn the other cheek and understand the richness of living. In preparing the self to meet the higher self one must learn to look forward to the meeting. When a child goes to school and does its best, it rushes to see its report card. The child, who has grand expectations for the mirroring of its performance, works hard at being the best he or she can be all the time. It is the child of woe who knowingly sloughs-off his lessons who looks to a day of requital with fear and trepidation.

This knowledge was acquired and taught to generations of the times. It was rehearsed and practiced by more and more people as time ticked on. Life had more of a wholesomeness about it, because it taught them they were it and it was them. It was good.

Chapter

16

SUCCESS

SUCCESS IS A VAGUE and nebulous term. Some of what the knower knows is this journey is not just an empty dream. It offers opportunities for people to transcend into better versions of themselves. These transcendences are deemed the ultimate successes. They will ever remain the only things that can exit life with a person. Everything else remains in life including time and the physical body. Transcendence is the prize awarded the spiritual body or the true self. Entrance into life is the beginning of ones exit from life. Success then may be affirmed as transcending life or reincarnation. Success at this level of achievement is The Ultimate Success. The transcendent version of self is the most fulfilling attainment.

There are many subtle traps in life. These traps are engendered to distract man from the reality of life being a learning experience, only. When men fall into life traps they stagnate and assume they have arrived at the meaning of life. On the contrary, they have relaxed and lost their higher purpose for being e.g. they have been distracted. In cases such as this loss of finding self is the price that a person has to pay. They exit life as lost souls and must return to life to continue the search for self.

What men will be in the hereafter is in their control. What men fashion themselves into in this journey is what they will find as themselves in the dimension to come. Here Man has opportunities to perfect himself by daily preparing for their departure. Striving to perfect self is the Path to ultimate success. This perfection realized is goal of the awakened ones.

By practicing self-restraint and brotherly unity one perfects self. To start this dynamo it is necessary to believe. Believe first in a Creator of it all, and second belief that there is something to come. Lastly, belief in the power in "doing unto others as we would have them do unto us." It takes a stout heart to launch oneself in an unrelenting search of the validation of these Truths. As one moves along faith grows and doubt flees. All men are given as much information about life as their parents have come by to share with them. At some point all of that must be put aside then, a personal relationship with God will develop. Knowing that can make the tests less demanding, or the danger less threatening. Spiritual success does not come without trials, errors, and difficulties. For the self is hidden amidst razor sharp brambles, treacherous terrains, and licentious beasts.

Initially one must struggle through the jungle of insanity, only, to find the pit of self-annihilation awaiting their efforts. Then, the cooling of sanity become ones guide through the Path of emersion into union with the ONE. The shelving of insanity is sheathed in the quarters of patience. Arriving at this junction of the Path one no longer walks the Path. At that point the one becomes one of those who are the Path. It does not happen over night. All things real take time. Restated it is the starting point of being and the ending of insane out of control behavior. It is the awakening to the self-destruction hidden in the pinions of insane life styles. It is acting out life in full consciousness. This completeness has come full circle to the discovery of finding liberation is contained in self-discipline.

As for those who do not believe, their time has not come for Liberation. They will return to go 'round again-and-again until the light of spirit is awakened in them.

However, for now more people are able to achieve Liberation due to the modifications in the systems. With the changes came the end of War. There had been no wars in the last one hundred twenty-five years. The zealots of power and control had lost their platform. No one listened to the clamor of those types anymore. They traditionally laid claim to knowing what was best for all while poverty and indigence glaringly stared them in the faces. Their bleating of equal opportunity served only to reveal their lack of efficient problem solving. Time had exposed the insanity of the greedy, and the privileged bowed to the sanity of parity, and equality. Humans were united in glorious fashion to improve the relationships of all humans and imparting peace to one another.

In this highly advanced World Climate the meaning of life was threefold. First it offered all people a place to practice caring for each other. Most had grasped the reality of continuing to exist upon exiting life. They understood unless they took the opportunities in life to practice things such as honesty, self-control, and other unseen positive things it would be the same in the next world as it was in the old one. Many found the rewards for this practice in mundane self-development gifts, beyond measure. They discovered wonderful things about themselves that they did not know. For others basic physical maintenance became routine activity and rewarded them with spiritual insights. Eating better made them feel better. This was apparent in the decline of fast food restaurants. Humans were feeding themselves and their children better diets. The obesity among young all people had dropped drastically. People were eating to live healthy lives, not to feed their over robust appetites. They were gaining control over their lives and it felt good. The major factor in the change in living was the advanced World Climate exhibited more sanity. It was more fit for human compatibility. People were more congenial to one another. They were practicing harmony.

Second, inventors were driven by earnest contributions to the human experience, in the new system. Getting rich was not a reason for inventing. Any invention, which required any part of the commonwealth instantly, became common property and each family was entitled to the invention.

The last of the three is the secrets held in Liberation. These secrets became open to all with the arrival of the new system. First, no longer were humans held captives of Fear, Safety, Hunger, Indigence, and Homelessness. Second, Proper Religious teachings and True Education had dispelled those ills and the spirit was nourishing its wards. Many of the harbingers of Liberation were kept in check by the new system. Others gave way to steady practice of doing good to one another. Last, all that remained was practice, practice, and more practice. Resulting in the perfection of sanity. Man had come of age ensuring Peace on Earth. Human being had found the gift hidden in "Do unto others as you would have them do unto you." It was the fulfilling of the Creators Master Plan, as all believers were Masters of Self, sane! Peace on earth was established.

"Convert the darkness into my guiding light.
Appoint me thy guardian of Reality.
Make me dust on the Path to Infinity."

Paradise . . .

The Beginning

EPILOGUE

SINCE THE BEGINNING THERE have been beginnings. Adam and Eve's fall from grace was a beginning. It was the beginning of existing minus innocence. Upon losing their innocence Adam and Eve became aware of their being unclothed. Before the loss of innocence Adam and Eve knew God, only, The loss of innocence caused them to know themselves, only. For they had defied the Word of God and caused themselves to know their wills instead of the Will of God.

Man lives everyday drawing nearer to exiting life and returning to his source. The higher purpose for Man's daily aspirations to success may be reclamation of his innocence. In Man's return to source is an enemy Satan. Man has an advisor who will skillfully guide him when he listens.

Somewhere along the way a kind of energy emerged that was not of spirit. It became mankind. It had the capabilities of Man except two; it was incapable of believing in, God as the Creator of all things, and it was incapable of loving either Man or God.

It disguised itself as a man and mingled with Man as a friend and companion; all the while it plotted to avert Man's attention from his eventual return to his Creator, and his faith in Him. It was devious and constantly plotted against Man. It was the reason Man fell from grace. It introduced Man to forms of function as Reality. It tricked Man into pursuing fame and fortune as the ultimate successes this life held. It enticed Man to use falsehood to further the aims it had oriented him to chase. It is still sticking around today.

Every since the creation of Man it moved among Men Pretending to be his helper. Under this guise it is ever misleading Man from his purpose for being Human.

It knew itself and it knew that Man did not know himself. It is possible that Man can and will see the error of his ways and abandon the courtship of this energy and reclaim his rightful place in the creation. His hope rests in his reclamation of innocence. This achieved will restore Man to the bliss that was lost, and put the energy that is not of spirit in neutral.

This is the Holy War that will serve as the Ultimate Jihad. The war for reinstatement does not hinge on Man fighting Man. It is solely Man Mastering Self, and doing unto others . . .

The only way to be is to begin and ever after begin.

Peace Be with You
. Acker

GLOSSARY

Advanced Culture Any Culture, past or present, that holds human entitlements such as basic food, adequate clothing, accommodating shelter, or sufficiency of shelter, medical, an annual stipend for life, and safety, e.g a very strict Criminal Justice System, as the sole responsibility of the Governing entity.

Alchemist The mystical level of Islam known as Sufism. Muslims who achieve this level turn the touches of life into spiritual Goal, i.e the ups and downs.

Animism The belief life is in all things, and all life is connected by a single spirit or soul. Primarily, ancestral as the initial *Being* from which all else originated, exists, and returns to, GOD.

AVS Audio-Visio Screen

Backward Culture Any Culture exploiting people for the above human entitlements. Any culture that promotes competition among its people for any of the above mentioned human entitlements

Black Panthers A group of people organized to improve the living conditions of socially and economically deprived African-Americans in America. It was completely removed from the face of the earth in two years, by the FBI. **byor** Bring you own refreshments

Capitalism A very subtle and sophisticated form of slavery

Capitalists Individuals or groups who manipulate people for personal gains

Carnate Temporary existence in a physical body.

Child Abuse Acts upon a child that dehumanize and disfigure a child physically or mentally, Insane acts.

Child Molestation Acts performed upon a child that render a child an instrument misused as an object to masturbate with, using a child for sexual gratification, Insane behavior.

Colonizers Demons, witches, and warlocks.

Colonization Invasion of other Cultures or established groups of people destroying the Culture, oppressing the people, and gaining absolute control of the land, the resources, and the people.

Conceptuals Ideas or concepts that are fundamentals engineered to distract and confuse people about the purpose of life'

Culture A story being lived out by a group of people. They validate themselves as positive or negative by how much peace and harmony they promote not only amongst themselves, but also with others

Death An extension of beginning.

Democracy A social system dedicated to exploitation and materialism. It harps on delivering human freedom while withholding basic human entitlements. In a Democracy only the selfish, greedy, and sociopathic rise to the top of the society. It functions best when Government has become completely corrupt and depraved. It was used in the days of Rome and found insolvent and problematic in serving, all people justly. In part it contributed to the fall of Rome.

Earn a Living An idiotic term coined for Capitalism. What it implies is cannot be done. it is impossible to do this. No one can earn a living

Earn the right to be alive Living in a manner that shows respect for all living things and being honest, trustworthy, and strong in ethics, mastering self, needing no other government than self to do the proper things in life. That can be done by all sane Men and Women.

Education Formal or informal instruction in the art of self mastery. Emphasizing the relationship between self and cause and effect equaling the outcome of each person's life.

Employer Modern nomenclature for Slave master

Employee A human being tethered to serving a Slave master for pay.

Explorers Agents of Slave masters, trained in the dark religious practices of Demons, witches, and warlocks who venture forth to acquire the material wealth of others by merciless invasions, pillages and plunders.

Freedom Having access to all the rights and privileges available to people in a specific Culture.

Form of Function Items invented or produced by combining matter and energy which harm the environment in production and become obsolete in rapid or long spans of time, and eventually are termed trash or waste.

God Referencing the Creator and sustainer of the Universes. Allah, Krishna, Brahma, Jesus, Jehovah, Elohim, Yhwh, Yahweh, Christ, Ilh, ElH, Jah, Isis, Osiris, gender less, etc . . .

HE, HIM, HIS GOD . . .

He, Him, His The Narrator or Story Teller . . . he, **him, his** A person who is referred to as subject of a situation or condition.

Hermaphrodite A person who departed life so confused about what they are that the Creator returned them with both reproductive organs. They are not a mistake on the Creators part. HE merely honors requests. They are the result of the way they chose to live in the past life. They will continue to reincarnate in confused states until they submit their wills to the Creator of the Universes.

Heterosexual A men or women who doubt the verifications claiming God makes incorrect genders and regardless of what thought they may entertain, or what source repudiates the above, focus on exemplifying the gender role they are created in, sane behavior.

Homosexual A kind of man or woman different and apart from Man as a species by personal choice or selection, insane behavior. They are anti-survival of the human species by using their reproductive organs for pleasure, only. The prominence of this behavior has preceded the self-destruction of every society or culture in the past. In this regard it may be defined as insane and dysfunctional. The genitals are for reproduction. When they are used to express love they are misused. Lust is the driving force that prompts the genitals into action. Love has nothing to do with reproduction. Ask the Birds and the Bees. Homosexuals are misanthropes, (people haters).

Human being Man an extremely high and exceptional form of temporal being created by GOD.

Imperialists The worst of the worst beings: Wicked people who do unto others that which they would never enjoy others doing to them. Thereby, they have dual standards and identify themselves as false be they King, Queen, or rabid Mongrel.

Inefficacious Incapable of producing a consistent state of harmony among human beings.

Innocence An awarded level of being wherein individuals have divorced themselves from manipulating others for personal gain.

Job A word for the duties performed by the Slaves in perpetuation of the Slave master's rich style of living.

KKK or Ku Klux Klan A subversive organization founded in 1866 by confederate soldiers to harass, lynch, and terrorize freed slaves. In its history, it has never been investigated thoroughly enough to remove it or stop it from operating.

Liberation Attaining the level of consciousness where a person transcends life's touches, experiencing victimization die to circumstances or conditions, finding union with God. The ultimate success is achieved when a person is liberated.

Man All people who believe in God.

Mankind or Kind of Man A type of man who is void of spirit, who neither believes in God or the hereafter. Who by nature is false, because he has dual standards, e.g. he does things to others that he would not want done to him.

Master of Self People who have as their mission in life gaining control of themselves and preparing for the dimension of existence to follow this dimension of existence.

Miseducation Education that is singularly focused on vocational preparation.

Money or Currency An amulet made by greedy deviant and depraved groups to garner unfair advantage and disproportionate distribution of the wealth, resources, and control of the Earth.

Parents Adults mature enough to be role models of people in control of themselves, and far removed from the practices of duality, i.e "do as I say, not as I do!"

Omissions Oversights in parenting, directly, attributable to structured social disparages, baring racial development and social equality.

Recalcitration Optional return to prison as a guarantee.

Reconned Strategically examined for suitability.

Religion Religion is another word for discipline. It is a way of living. People who practice a religion with dedication are disciples.

Religious Pertains to the artifacts, rituals, ceremonies, books, garments, and teachings.

Reticulouousness Mankind's inventive subterfuge of assigning value to worthless objects, e.g. gold, diamonds, selling land, time shares, and the concoction of the device known as credit, debt.

Slave Masters Generally, Slave Masters lack the ability to master themselves. Atypically they are individuals and all groups who bind Man in servitude using wages instead of binding Man by using metal chains. Their mastery of others usually entails violence, destruction of some sort, corruption, dual standards, coercion, law enforcers, secret organizations covert operatives, and violent retaliations against opposing systems.

Stipend A regular award of numbers issued to all people eligible to Qualify for Social Security Adult Accounts payments. Those eligible to receive the funds to have a card to facilitate purchases. The sum to be equal in all age group levels. Further, it affords people the option of using or saving and accruing their total sum of numbers without consequence or reprisal. Lastly, numbers may be transferred from an individuals account into another's account for personal transactions.

Sociopaths Greedy, stingy, colonizers, Slave masters, witches, warlocks, demons, and secret organizations who dawn suits, ties, including other attire of respectability to cover their dirty deeds.

Witch Craft The manipulation of people for the personal gains of individuals, groups, or Organizations, i.e slavery, wage slavery, colonization, exploitation, and miseducation.

Work Human endeavor that contributes in some meaningful way to the living conditions of all animal, vegetable, and mineral life.

Zotgram A hand held device that replaced the computer.